I0489128

Experts Share Their Techniques To Drawing A Vehicle

Master the Art of Drawing Vehicles

Vehicle Book

By : Gala Publication

2

Published By :

Gala Publication

© Copyright 2015 – Gala Publication

ISBN-13: **978-1522721673**
ISBN-10: **1522721673**

Table of Contents

BOAT

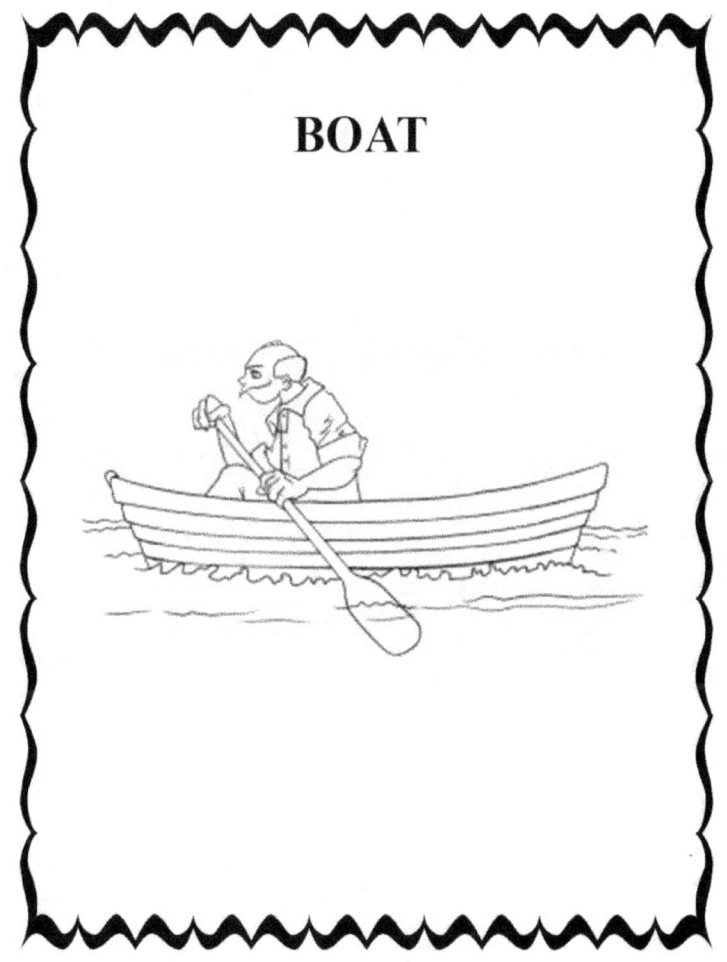

STEP 1

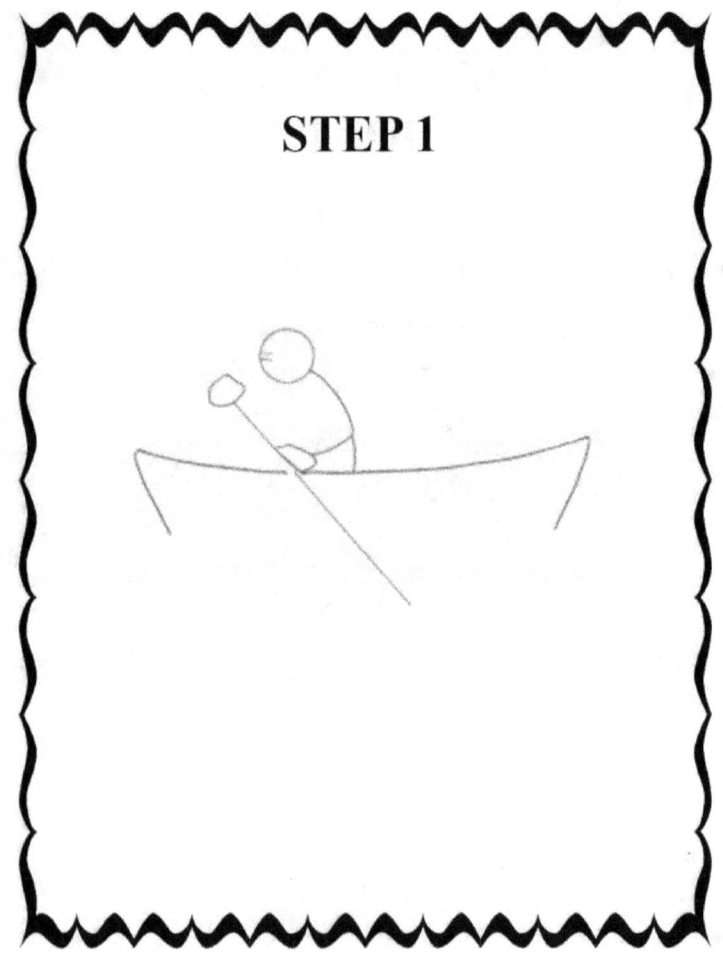

STEP 2

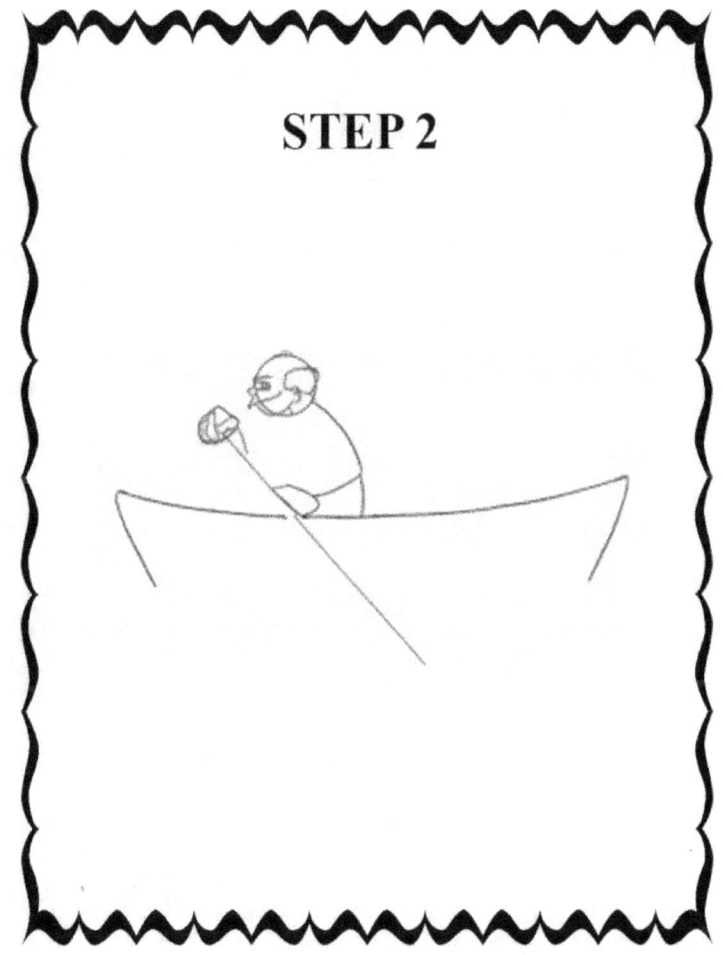

STEP 3

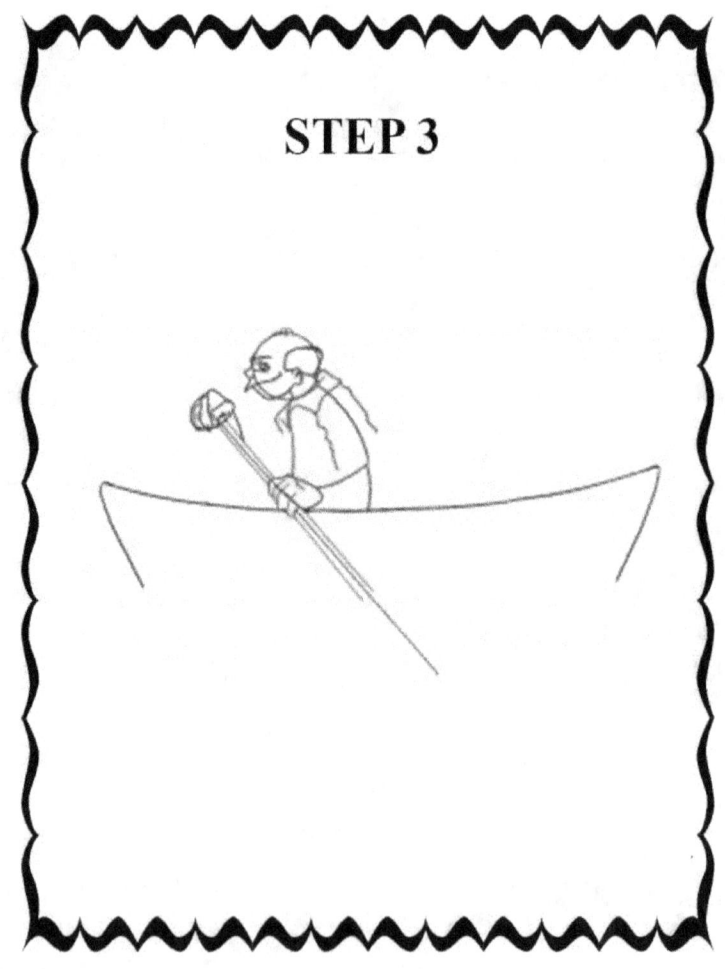

STEP 4

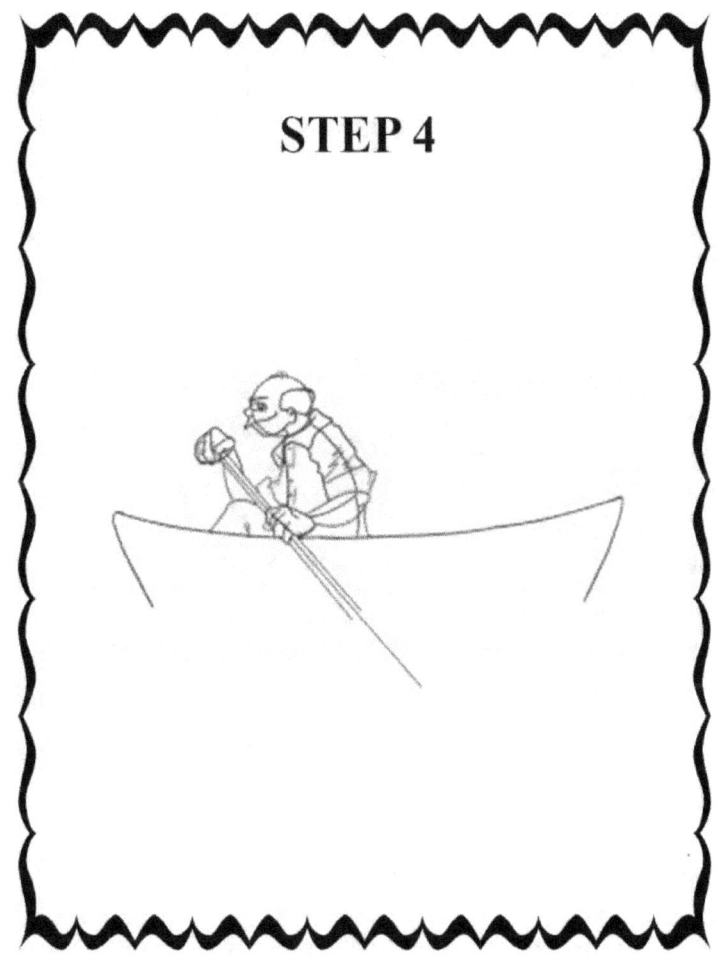

STEP 5

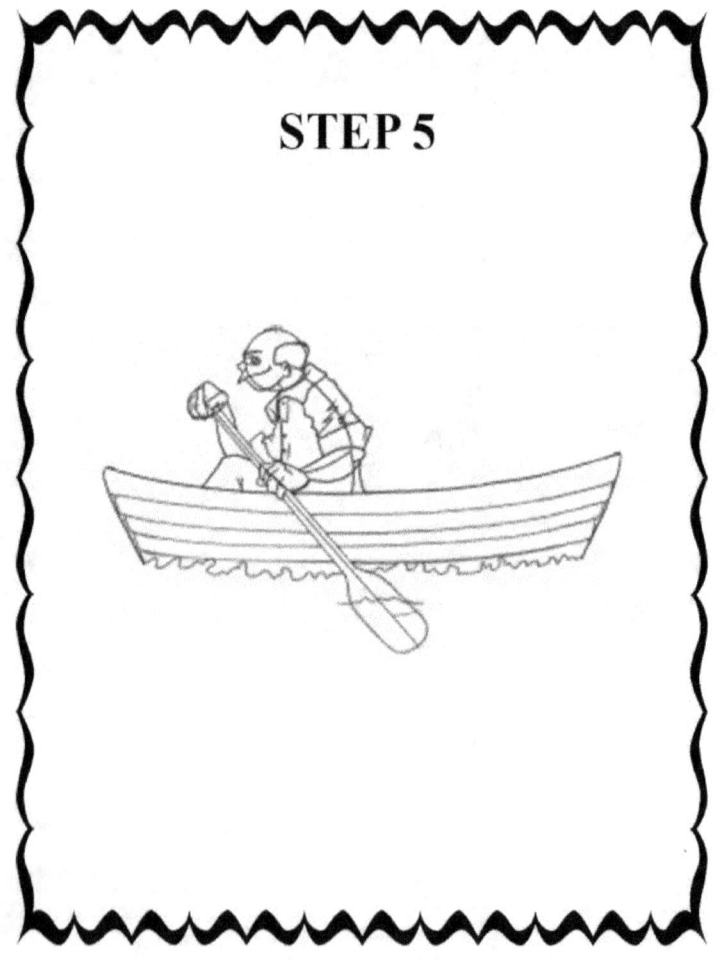

STEP 6

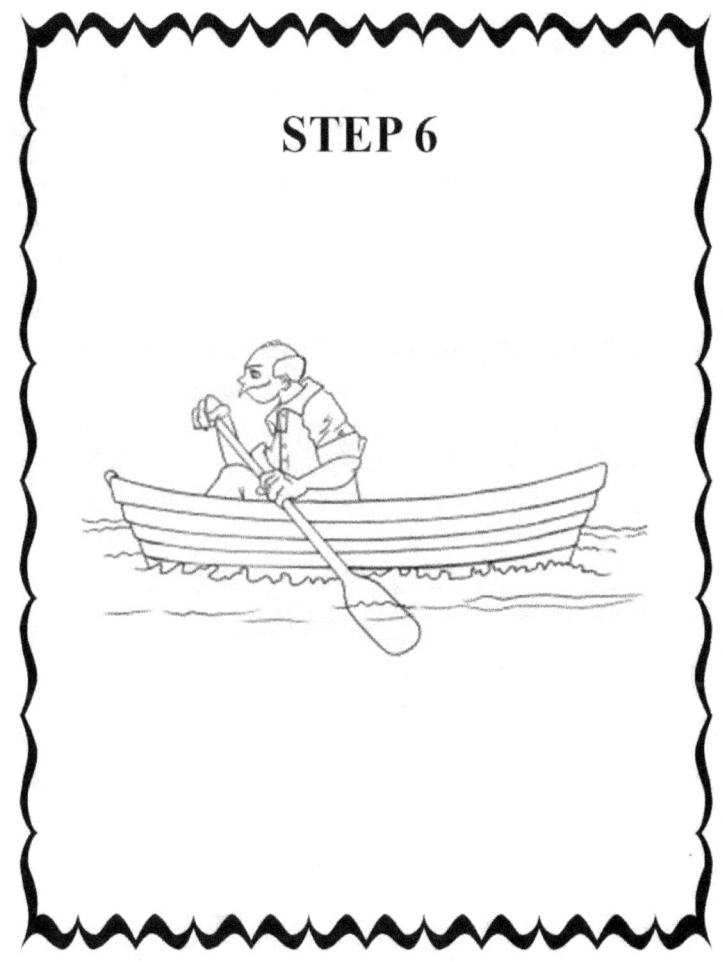

CAR

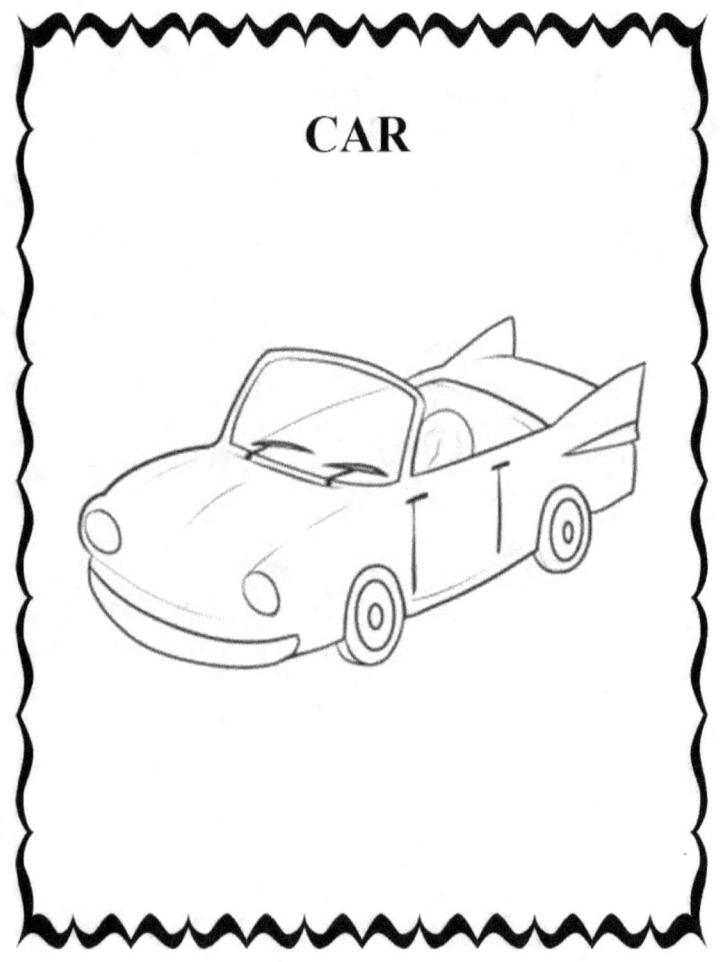

13

STEP 1

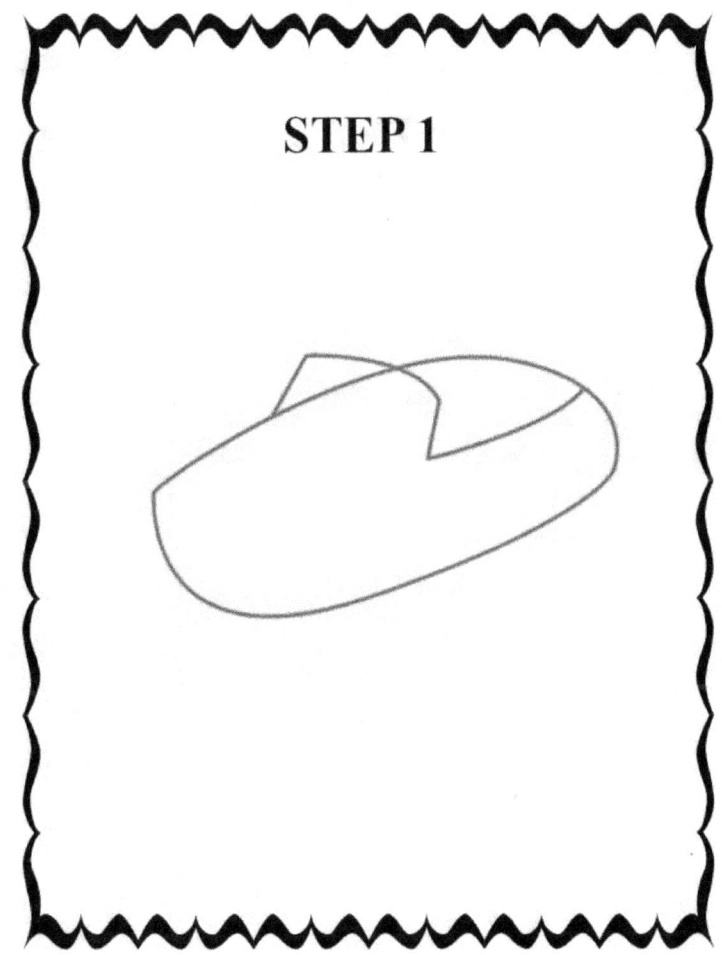

STEP 2

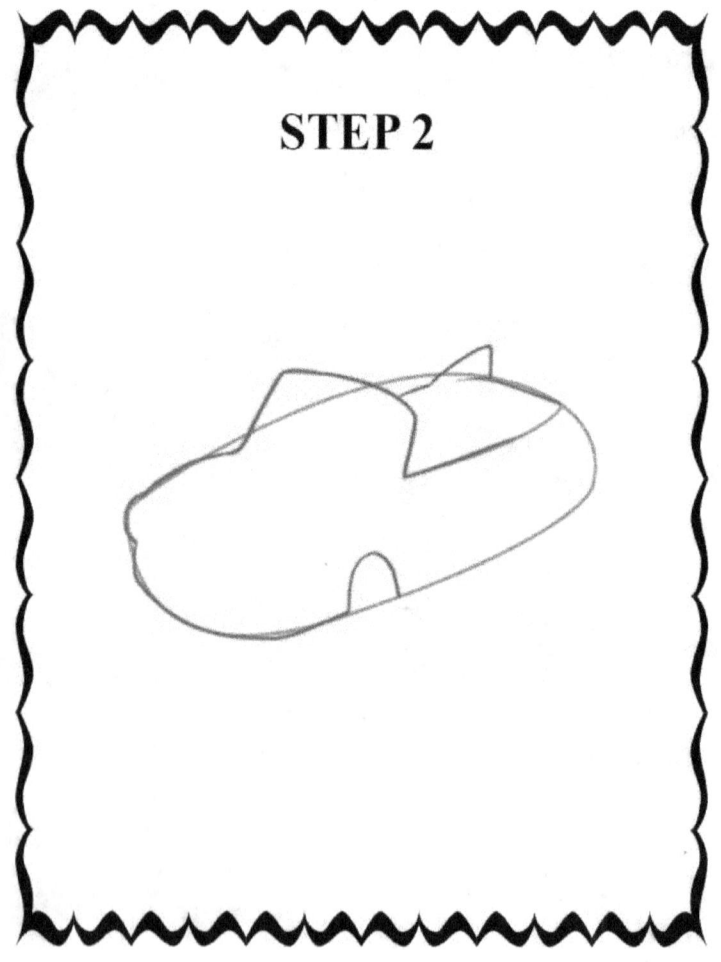

STEP 3

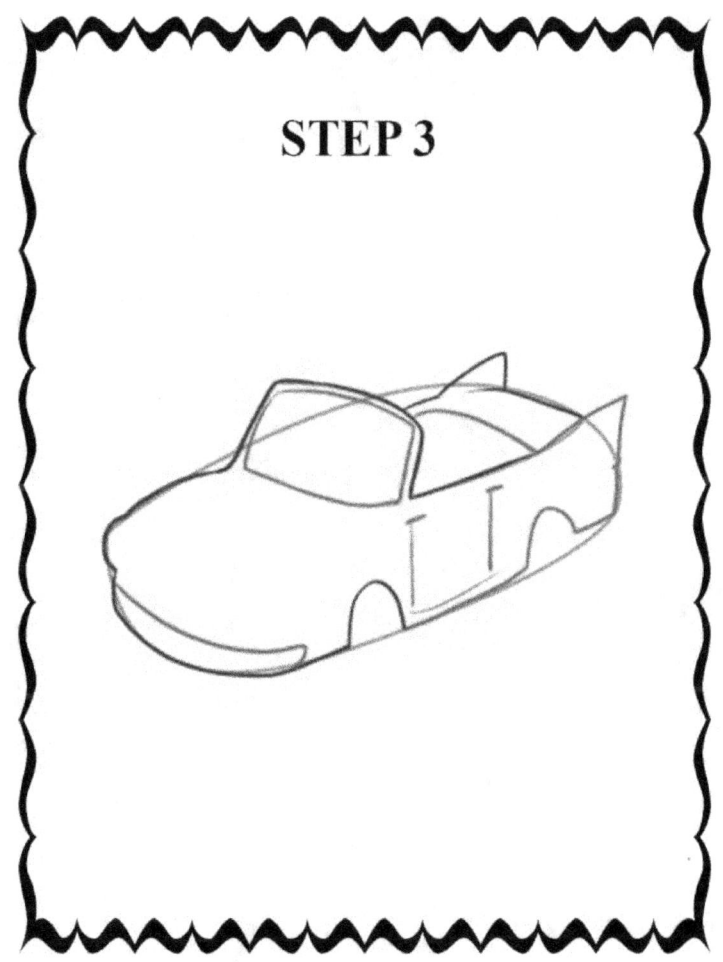

STEP 4

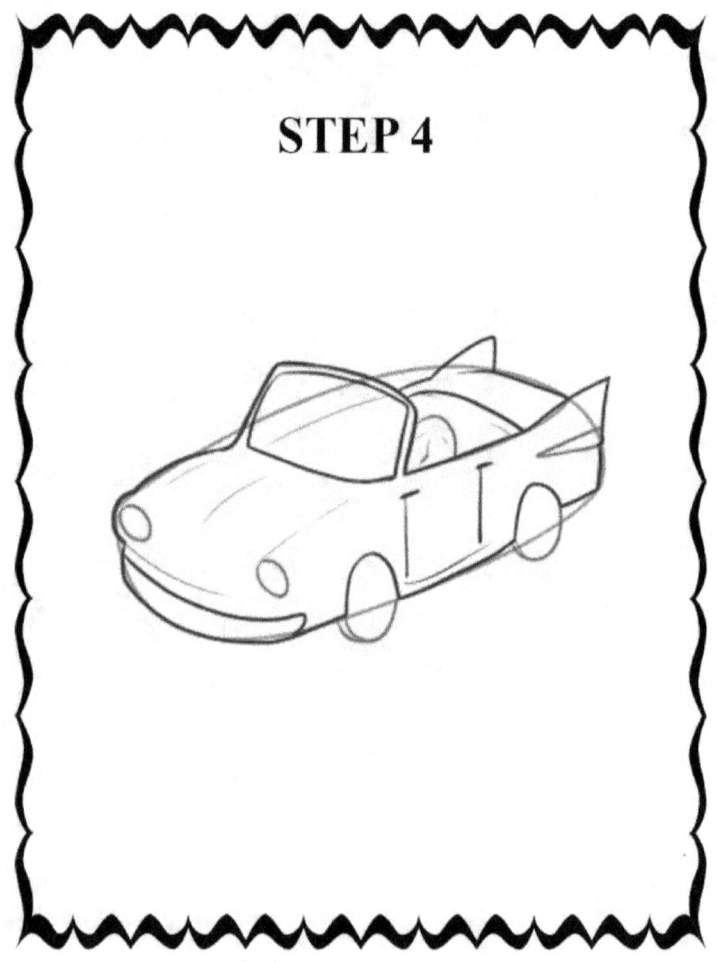

STEP 5

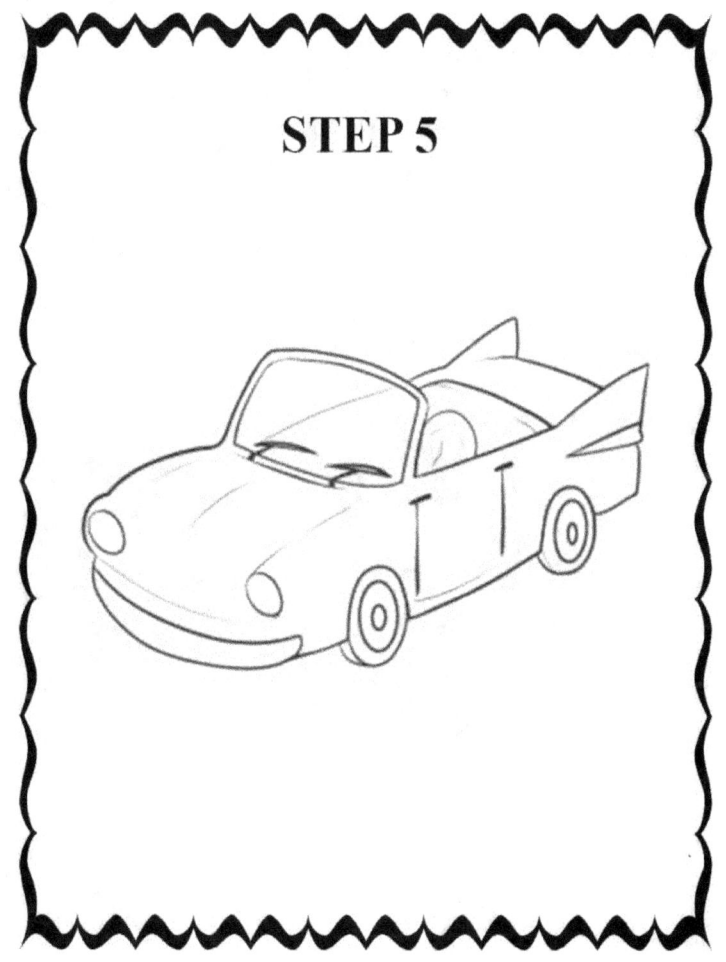

FIRE TRUCK

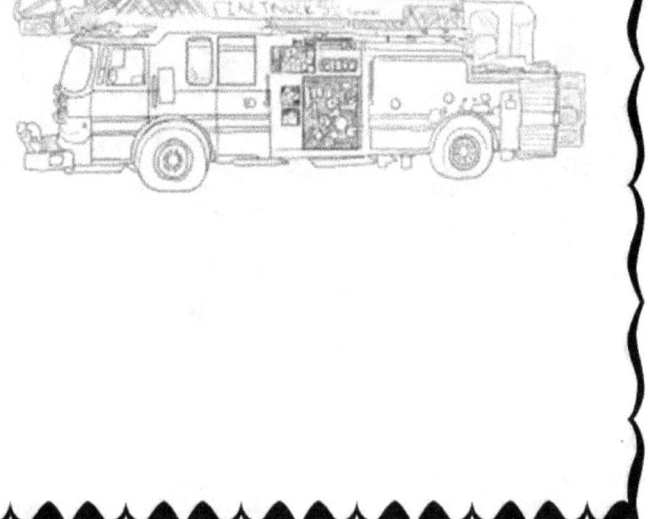

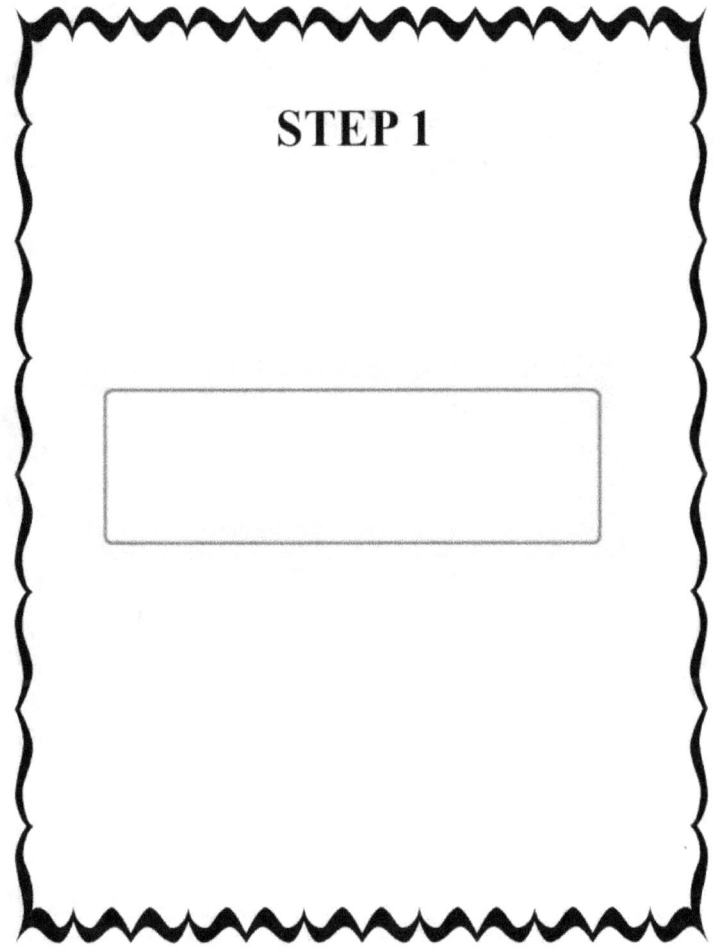

STEP 1

STEP 2

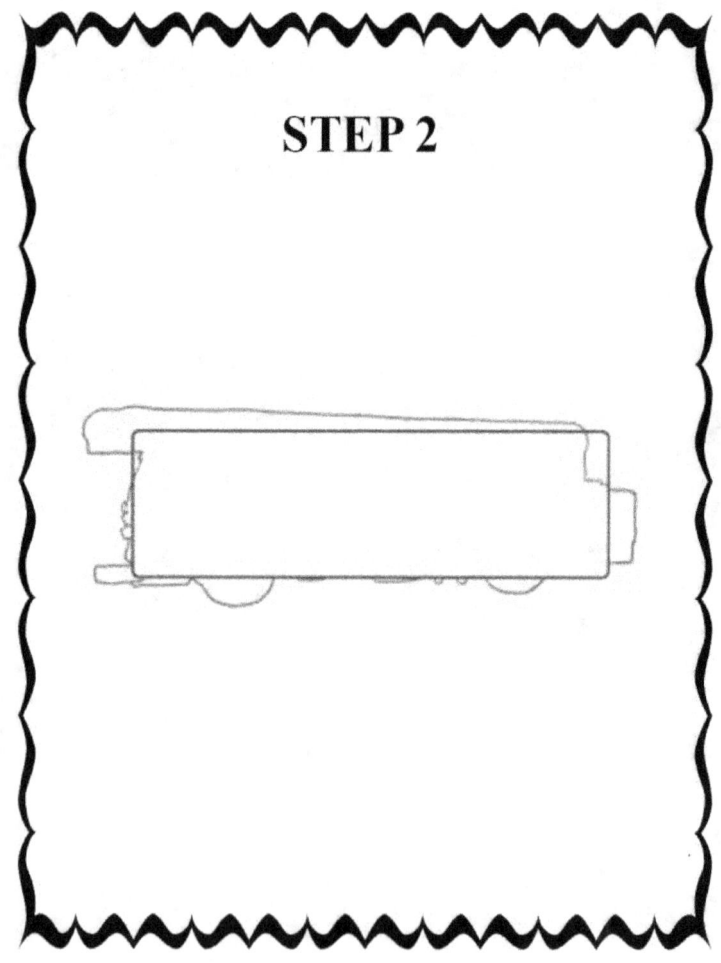

STEP 3

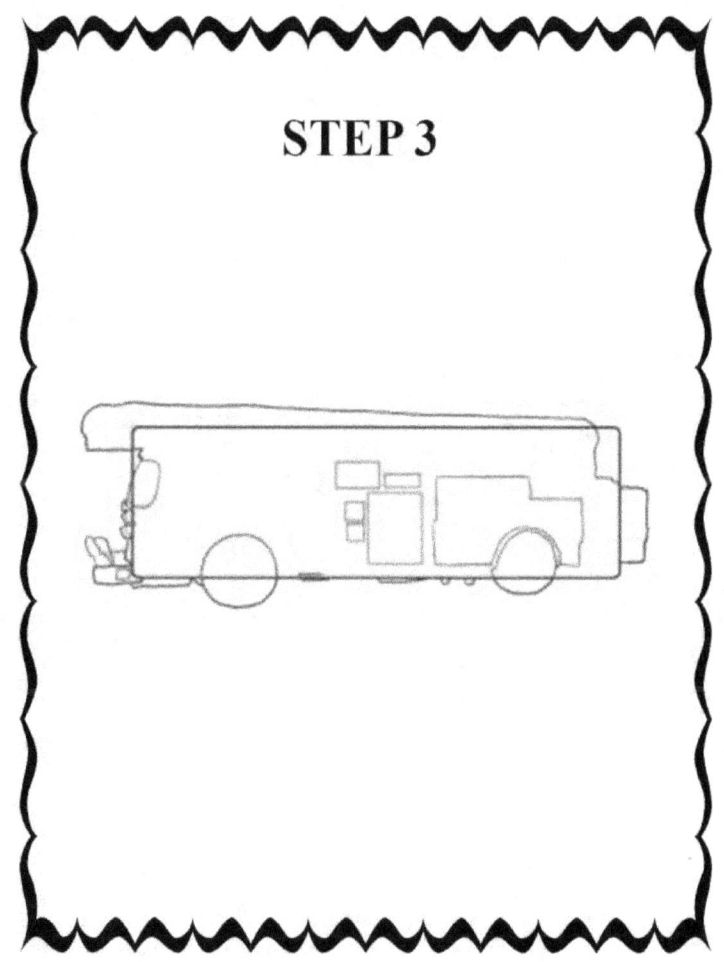

STEP 4

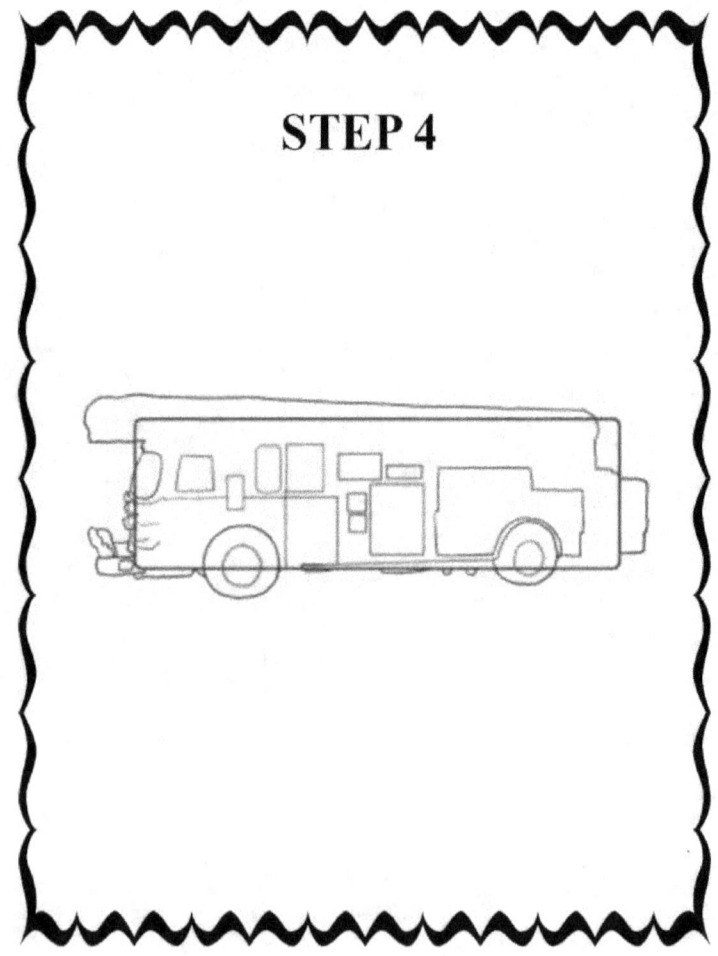

STEP 5

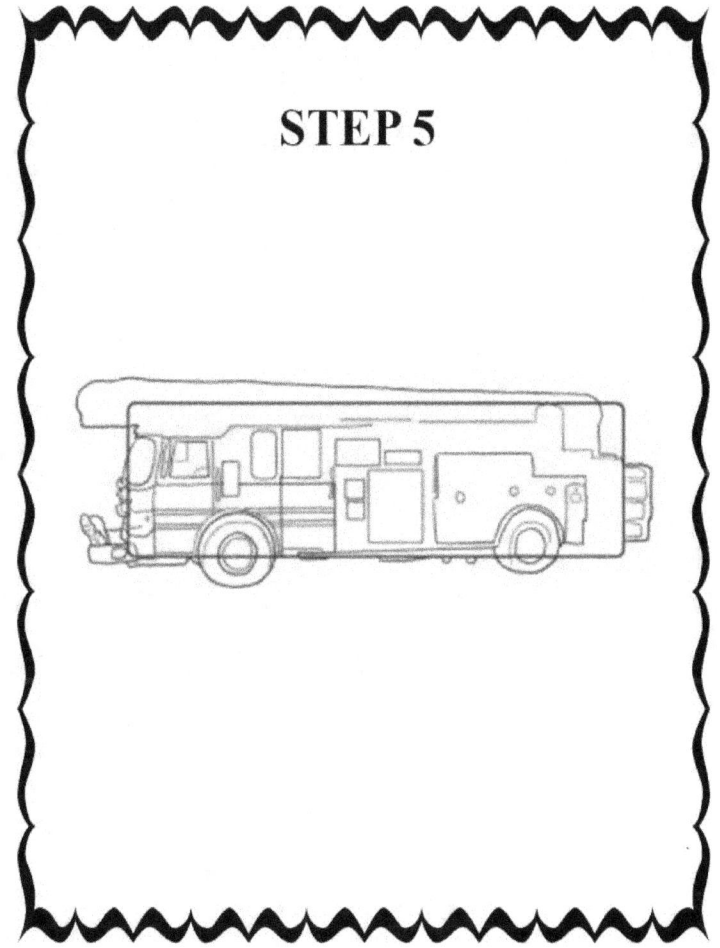

STEP 6

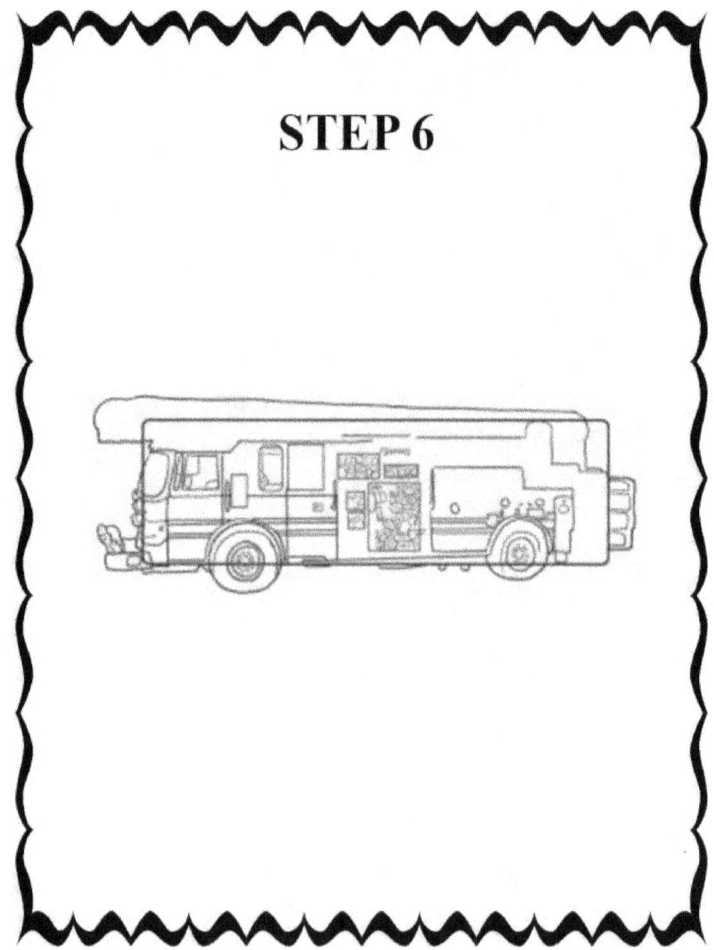

STEP 7

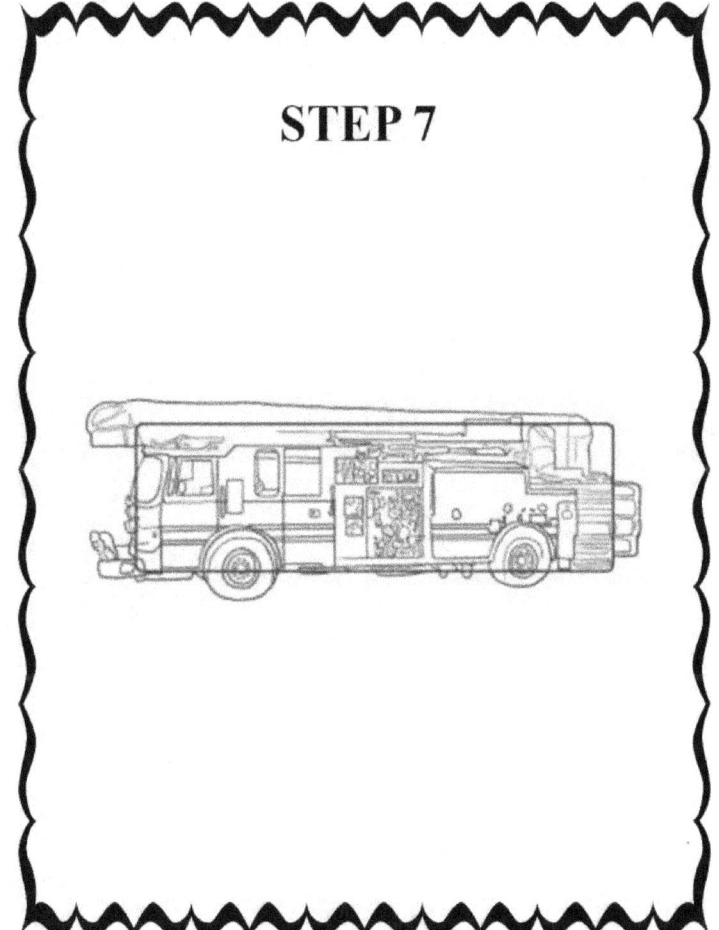

STEP 8

JEEP

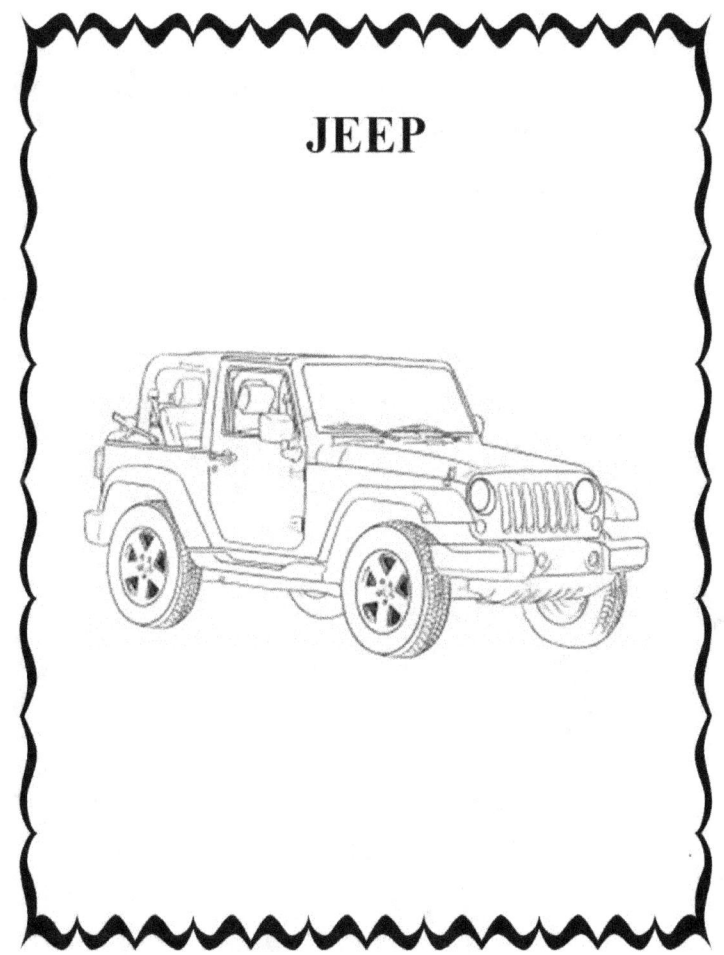

STEP 1

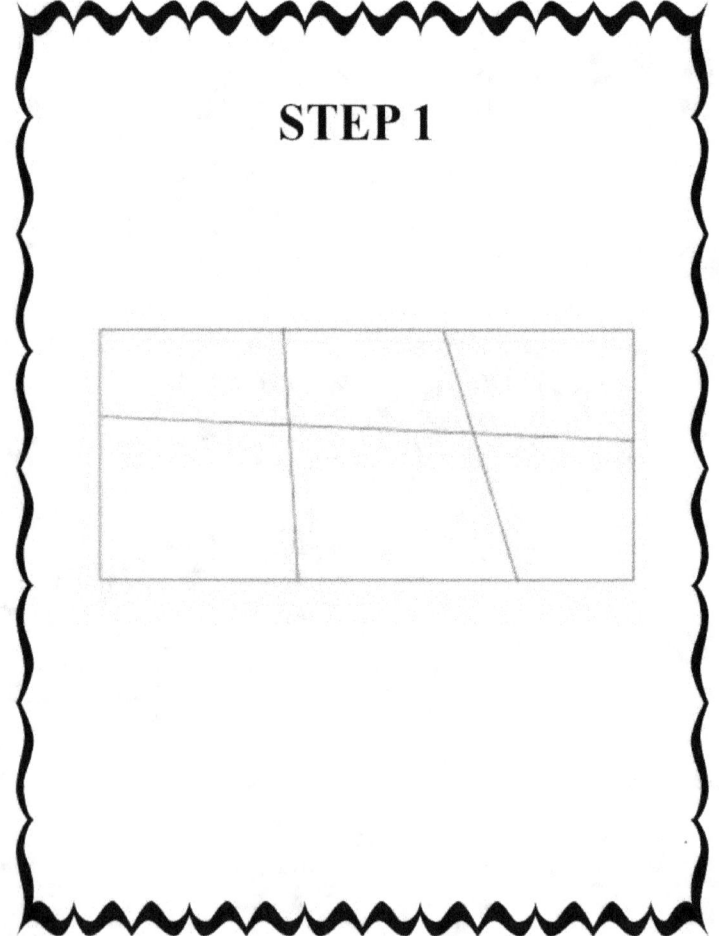

STEP 2

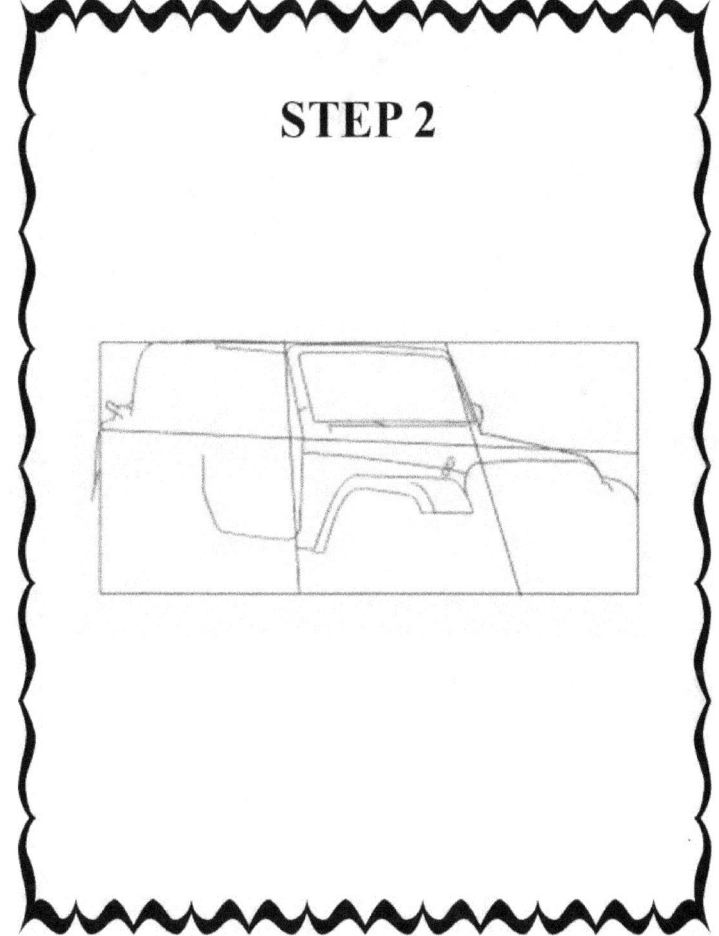

STEP 3

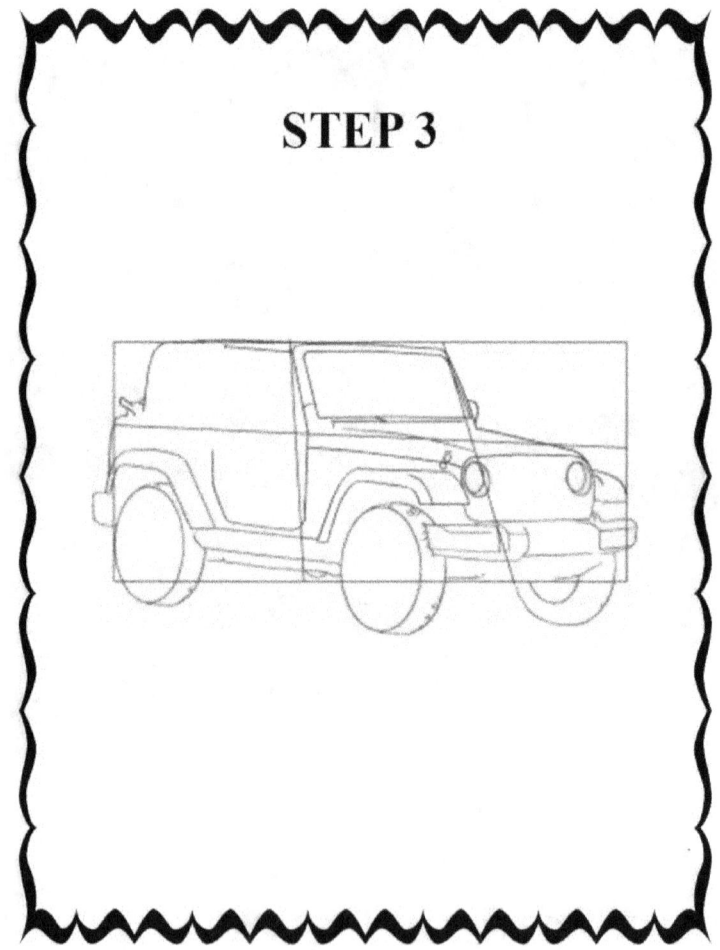

STEP 4

STEP 5

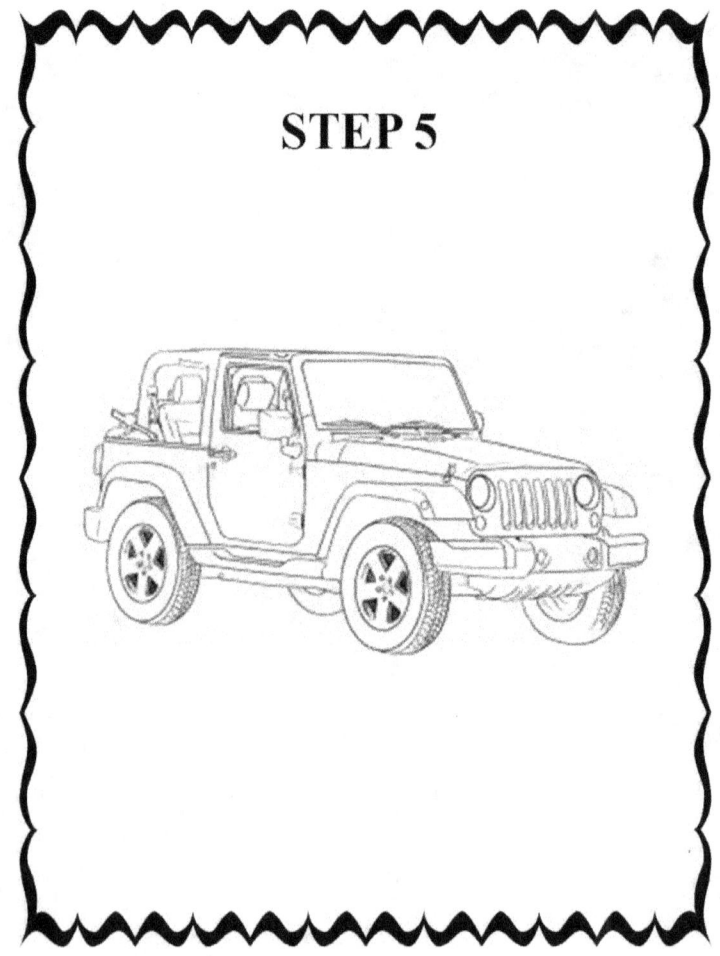

MAYFLOWER

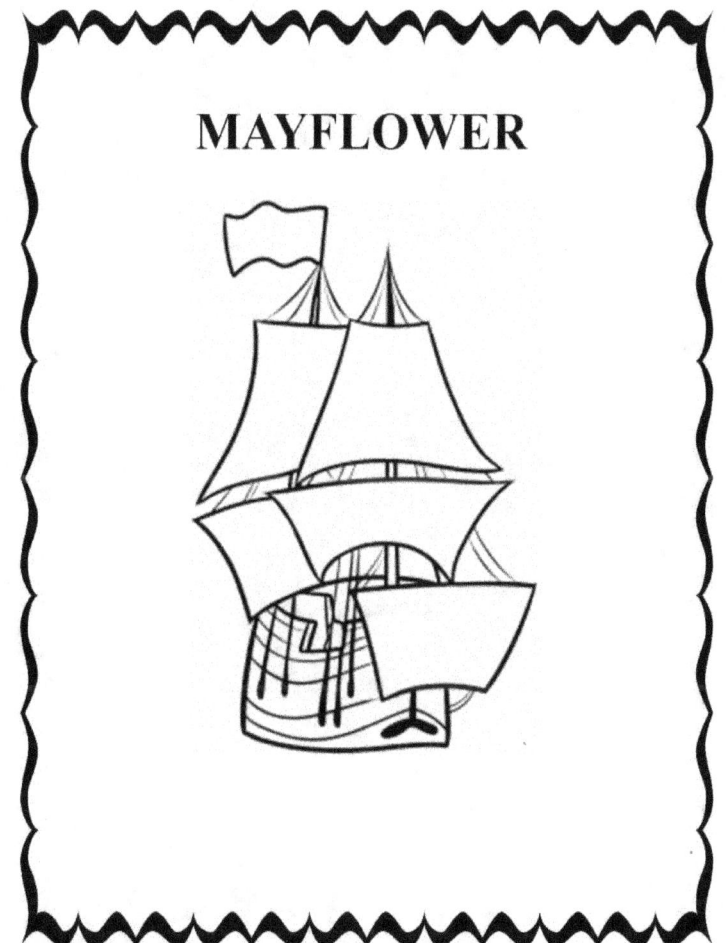

STEP 1

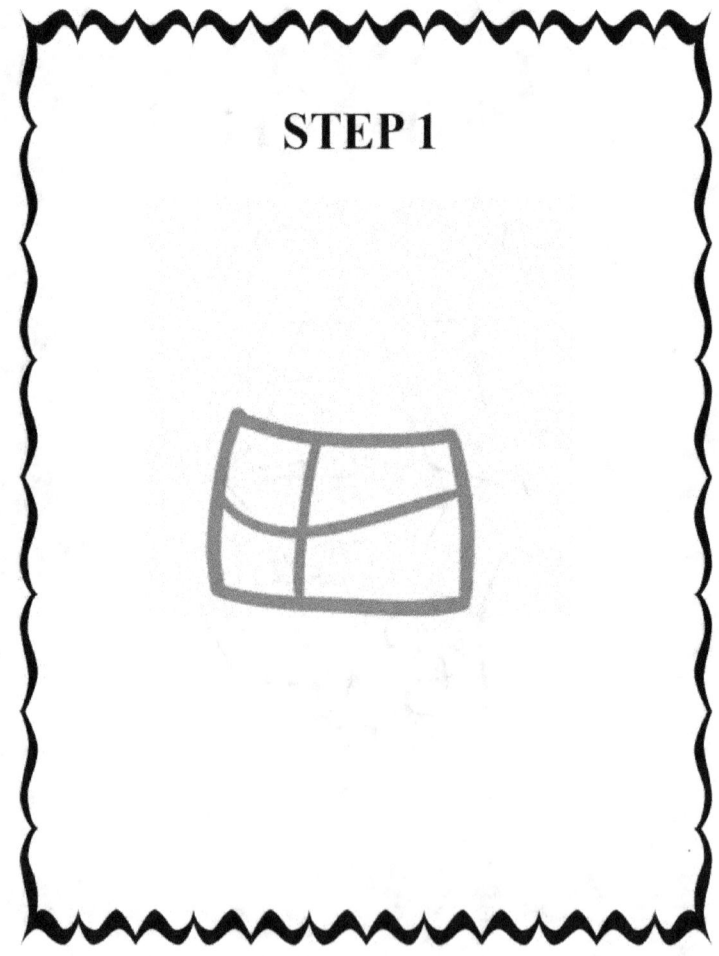

STEP 2

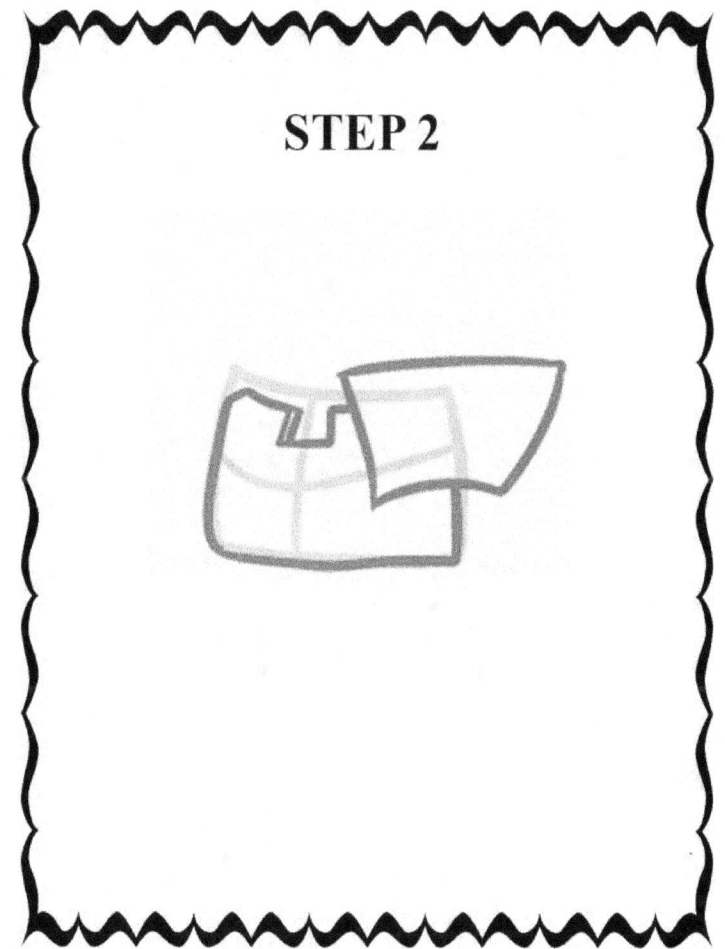

STEP 3

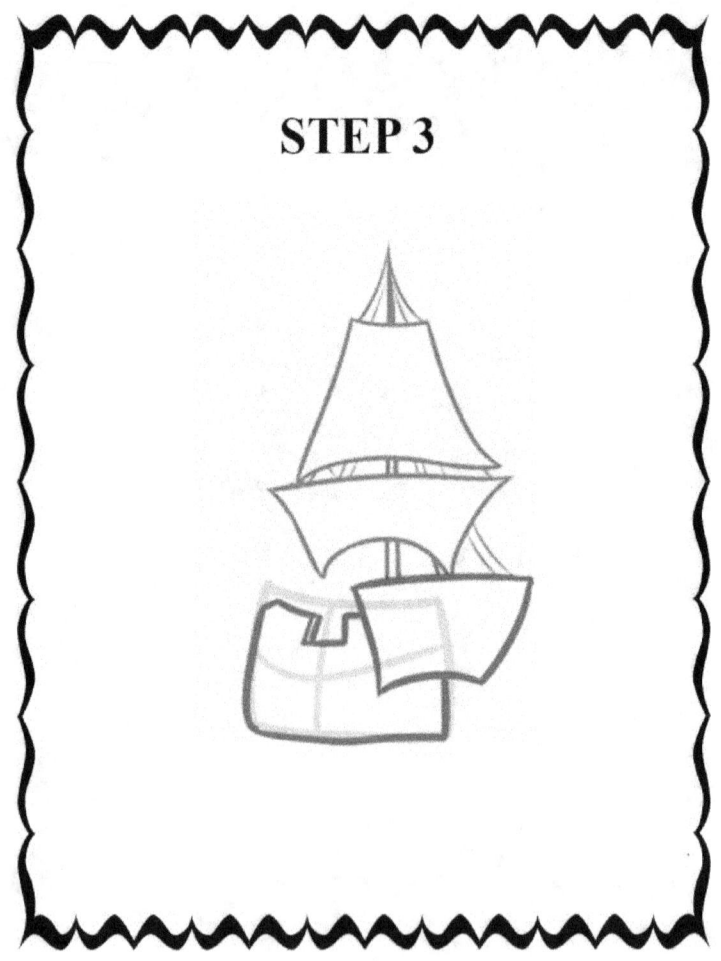

STEP 4

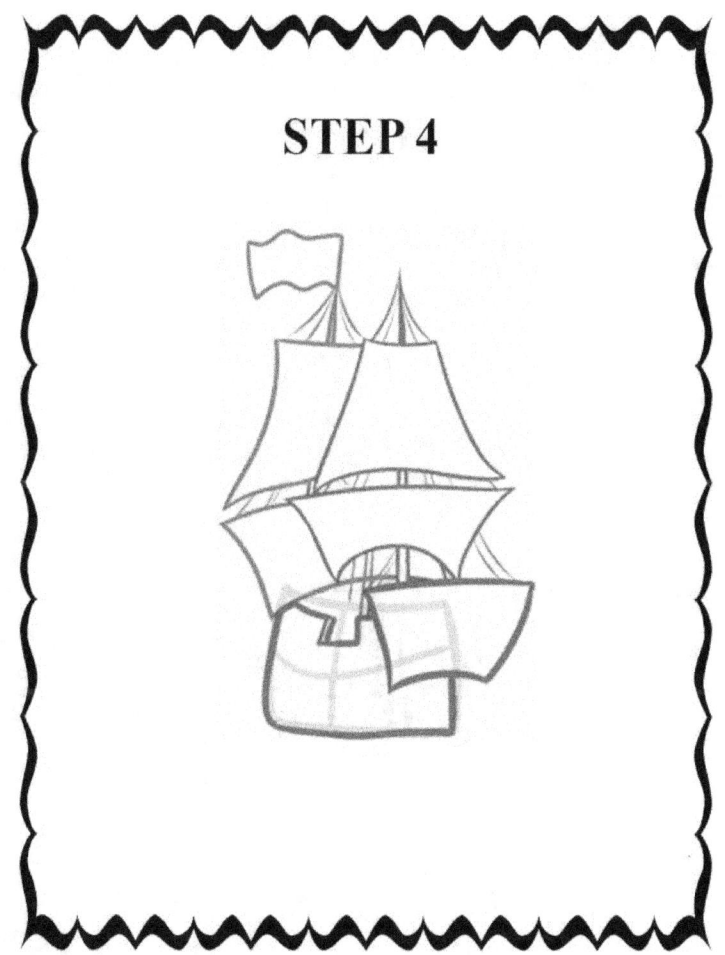

STEP 5

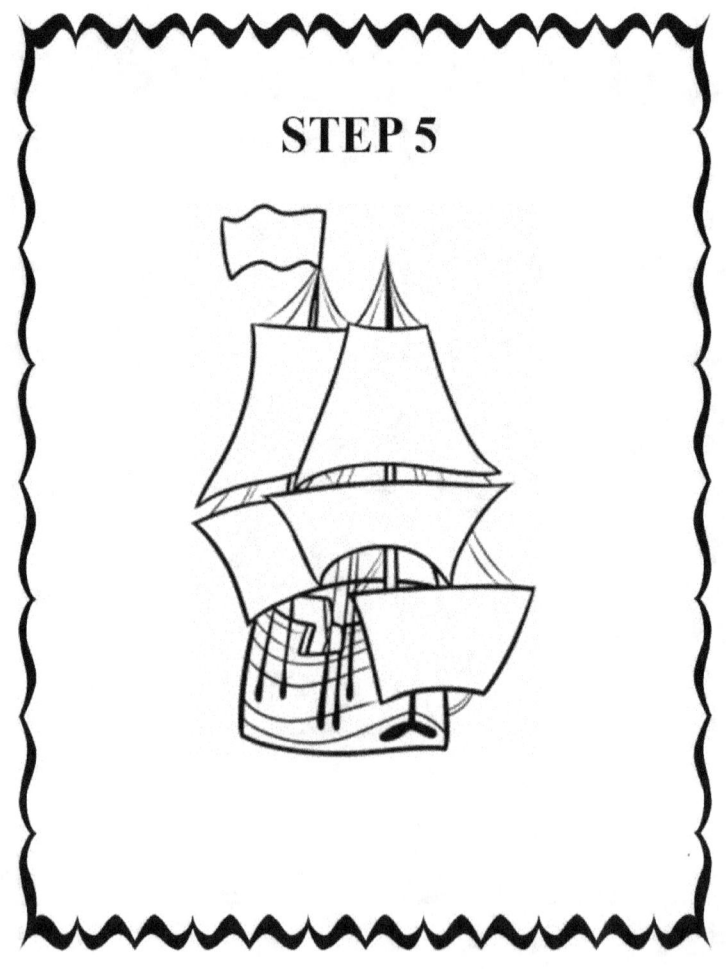

SAILBOAT

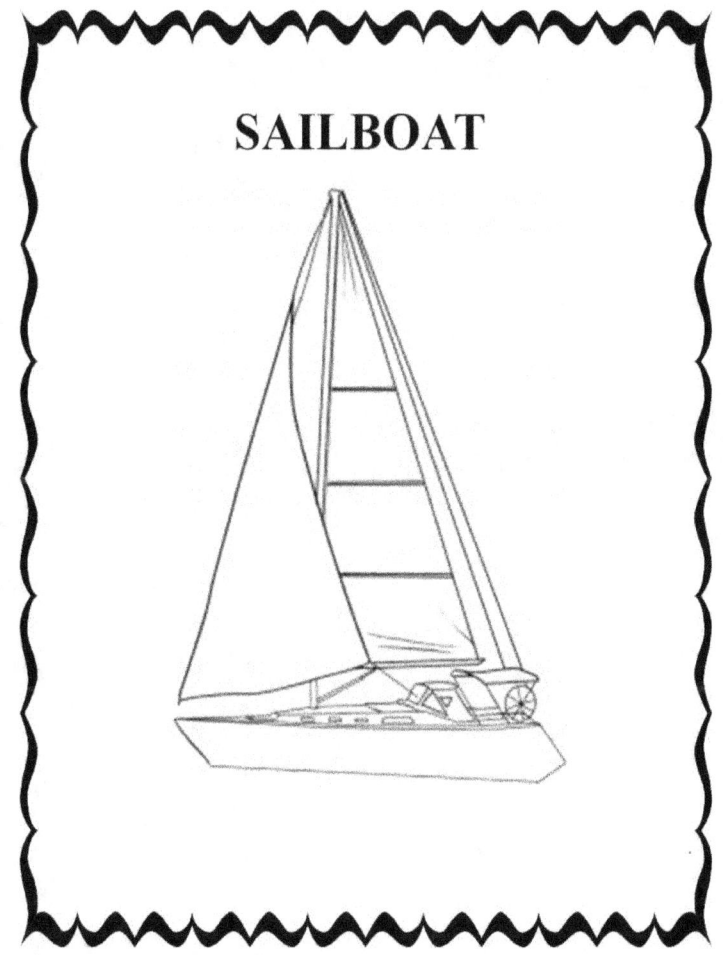

STEP 1

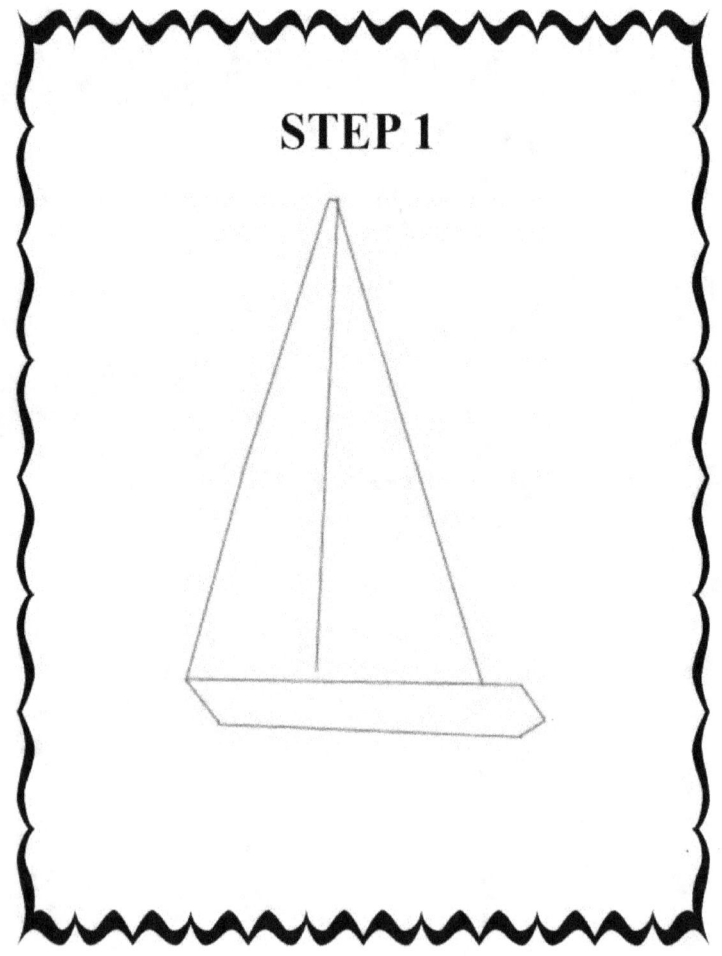

41

STEP 2

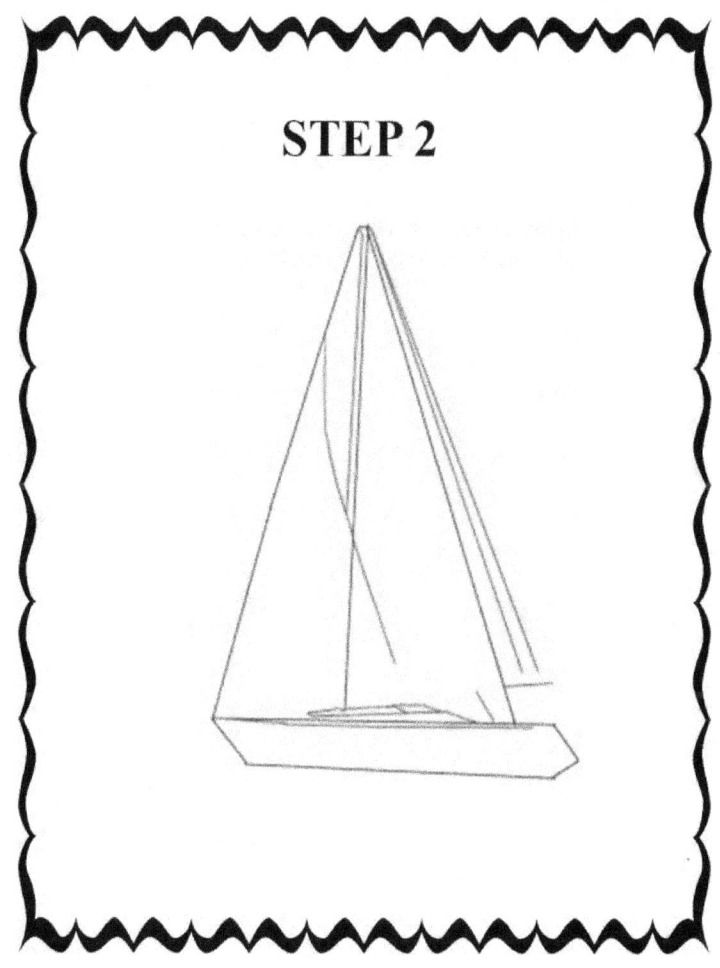

STEP 3

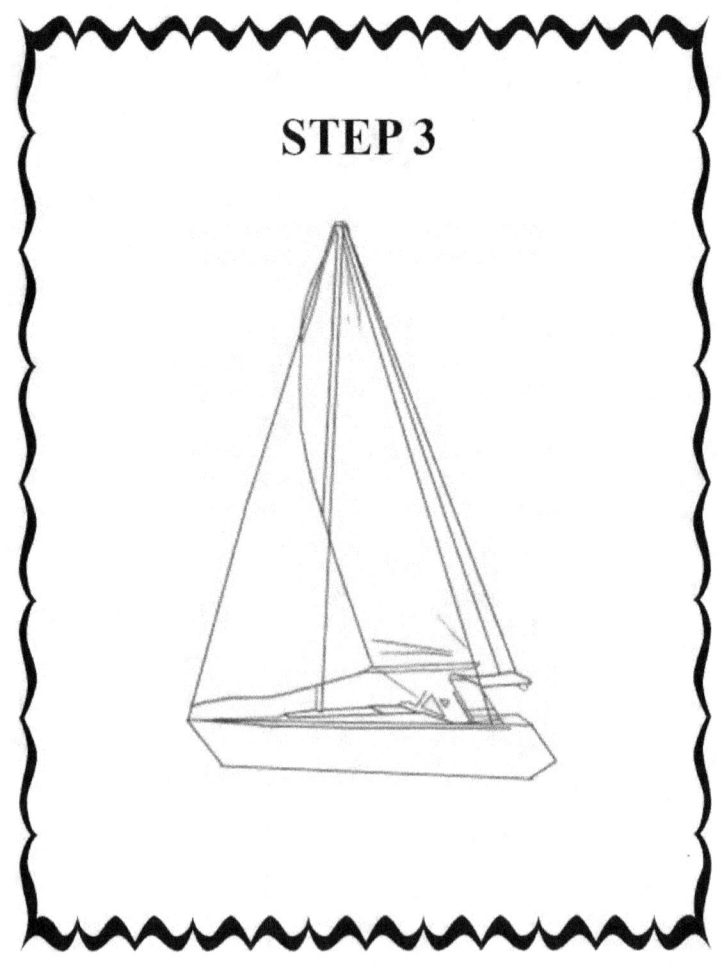

STEP 4

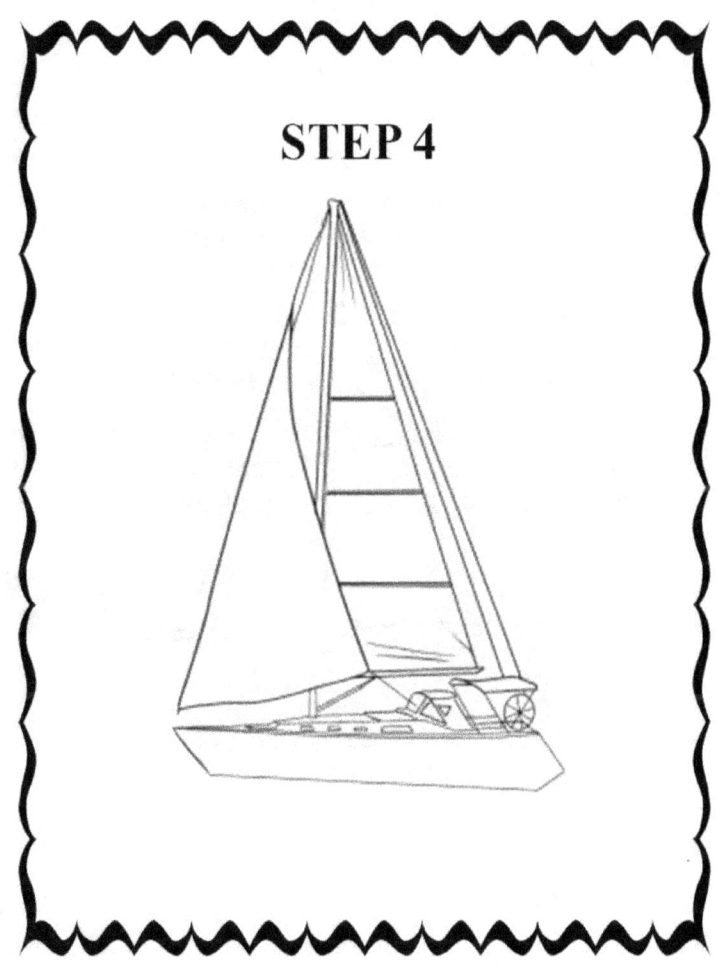

SHIP

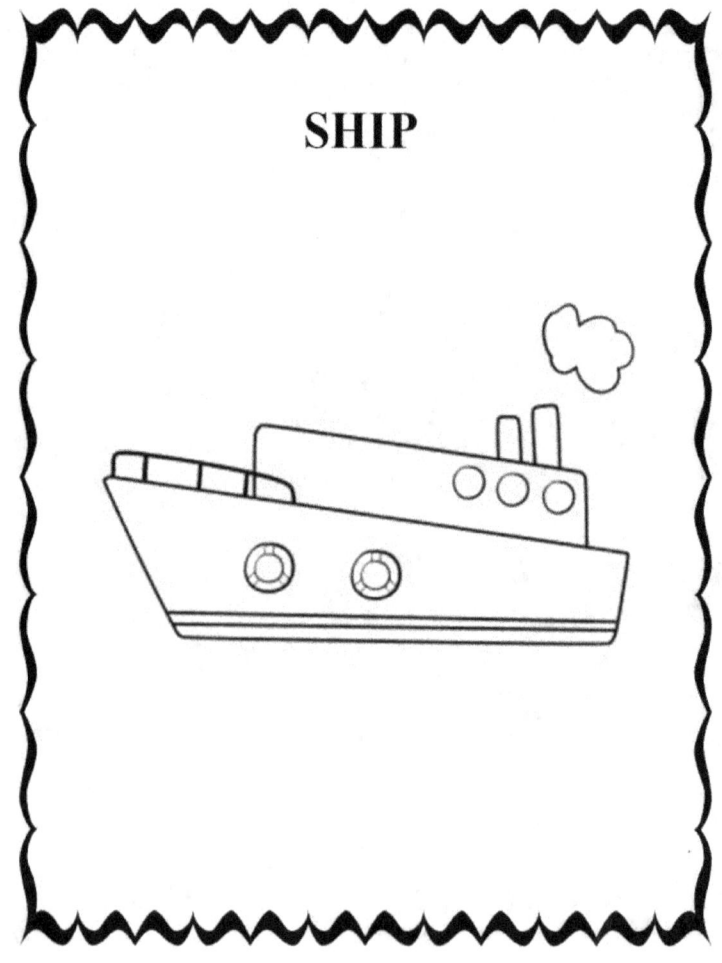

STEP 1

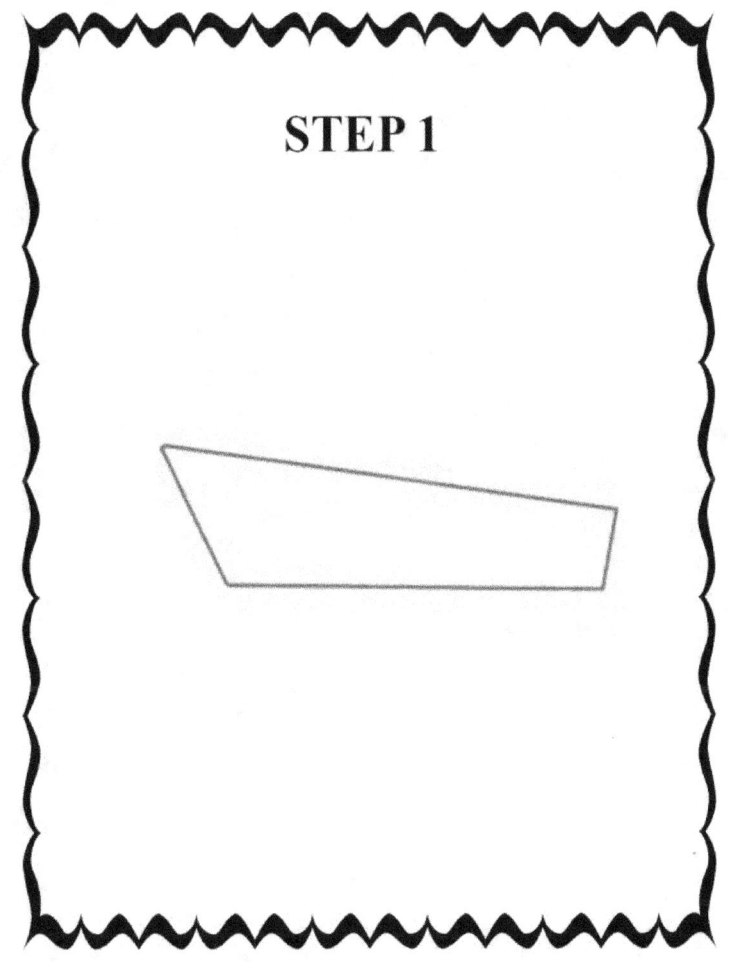

STEP 2

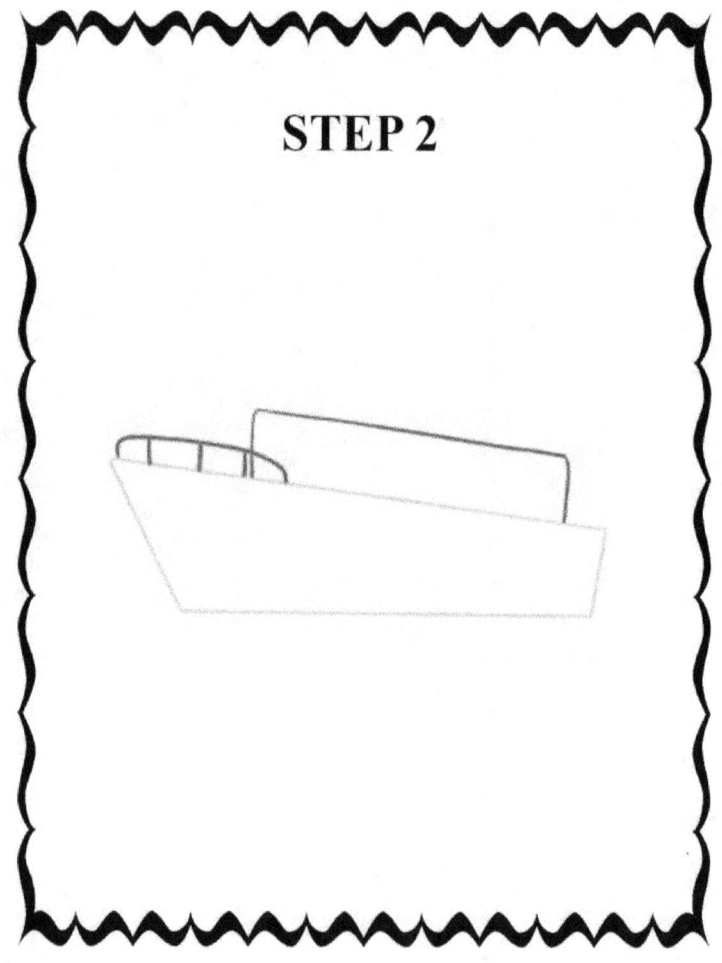

STEP 3

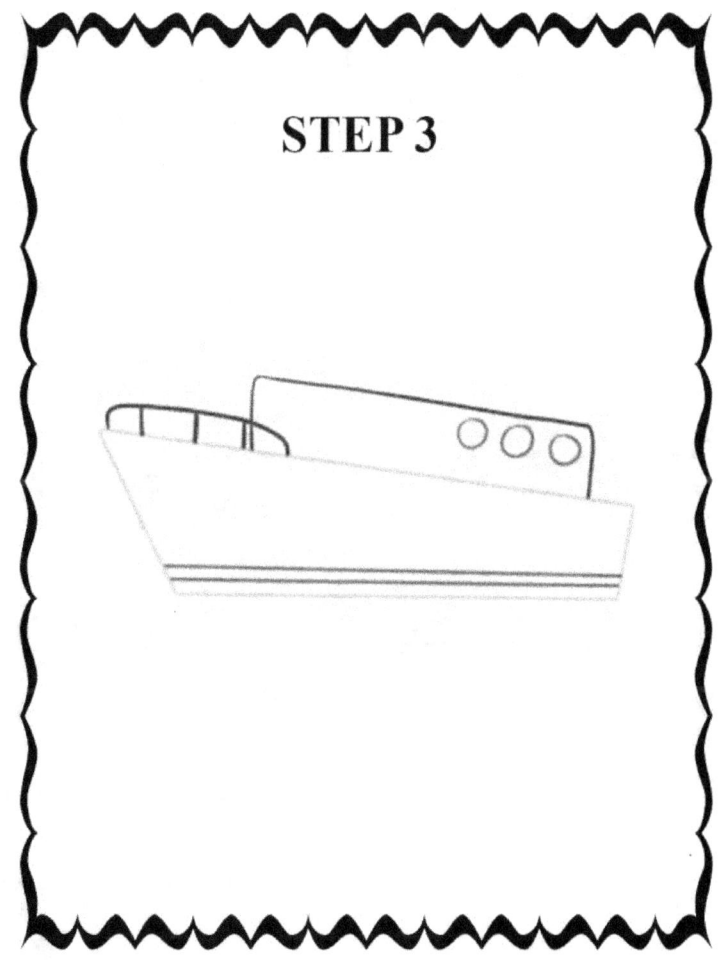

STEP 4

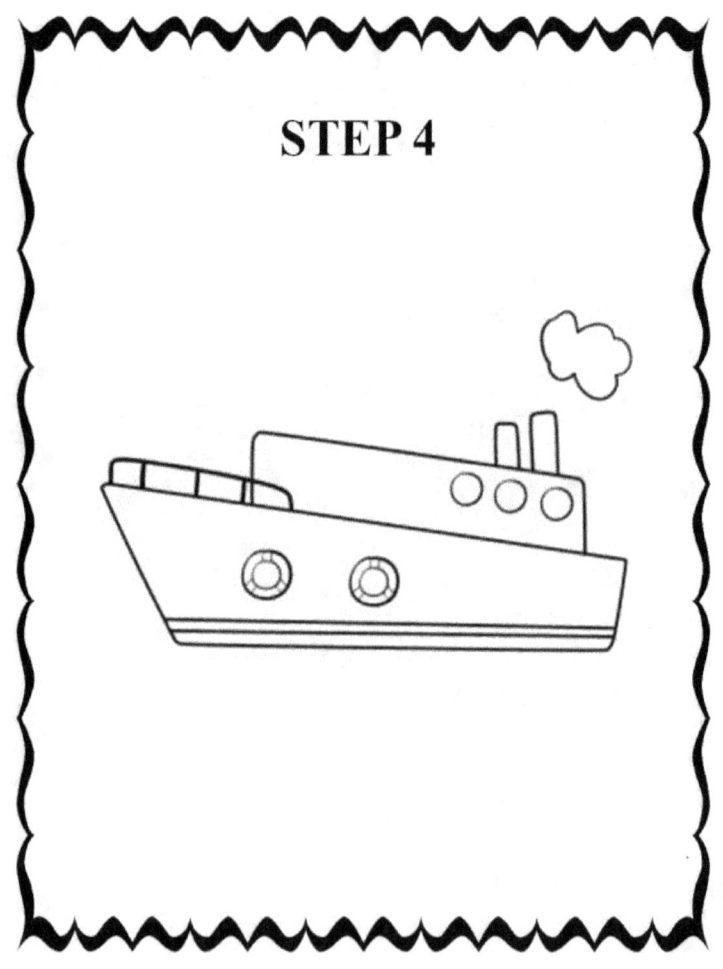

SUBMARINE

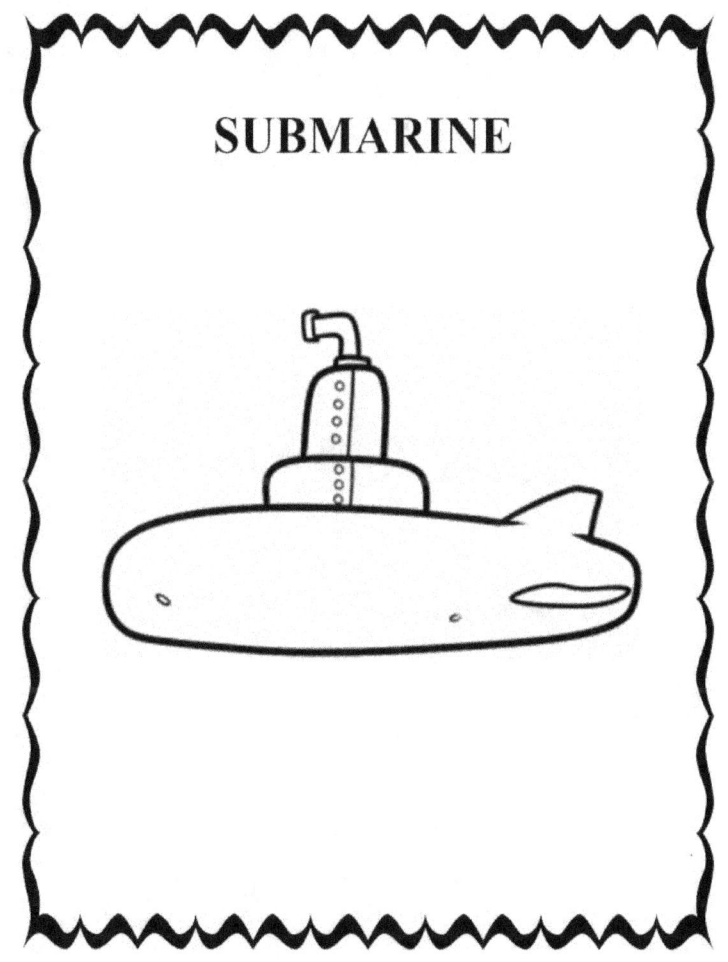

STEP 1

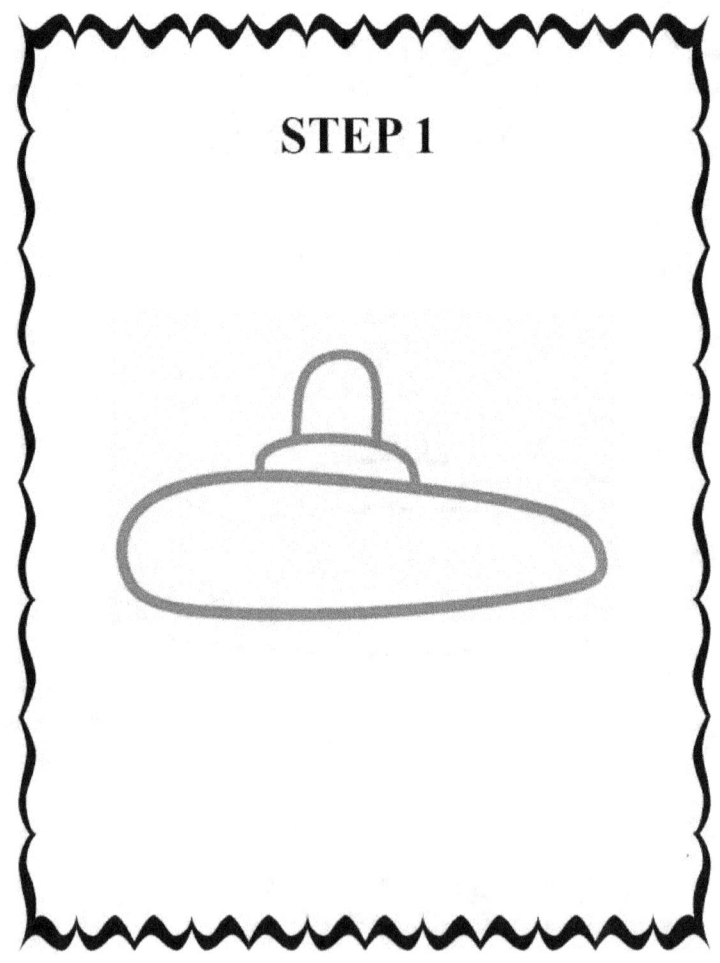

STEP 2

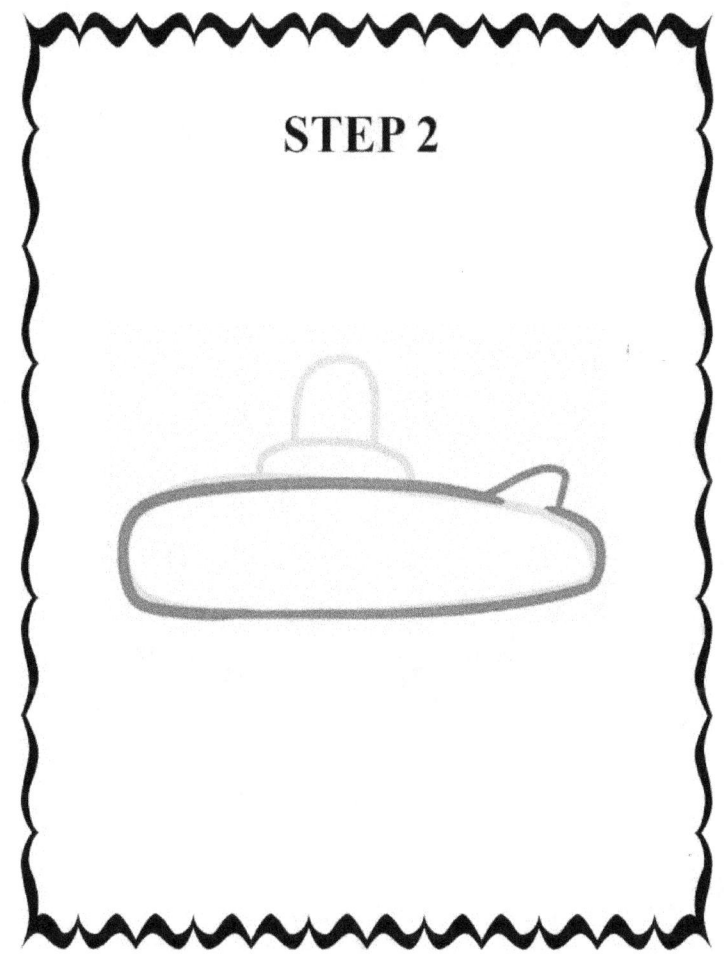

STEP 3

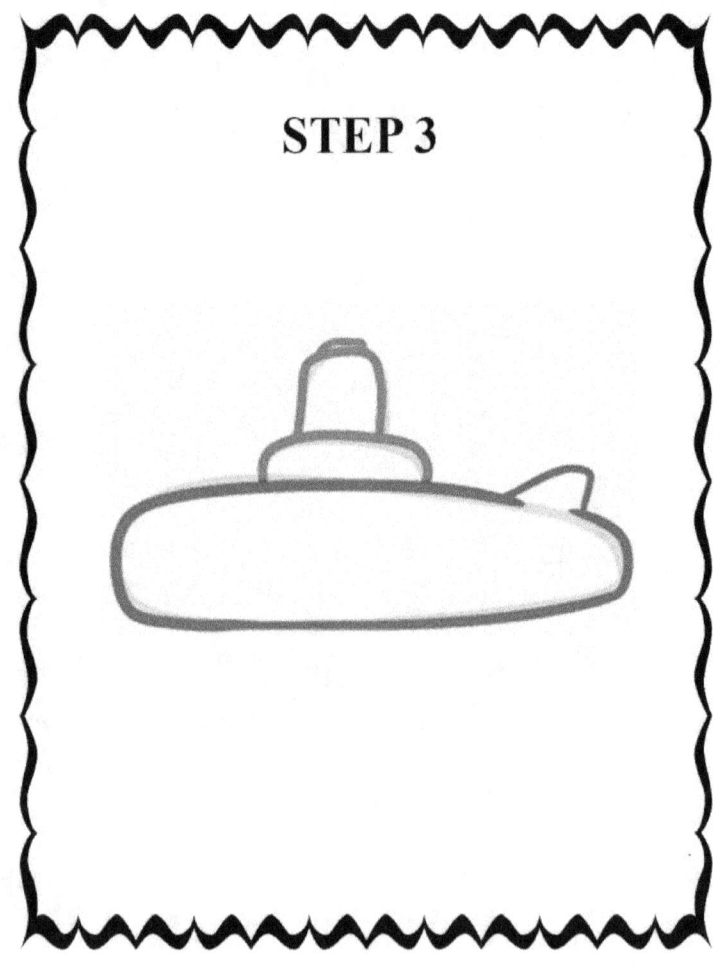

STEP 4

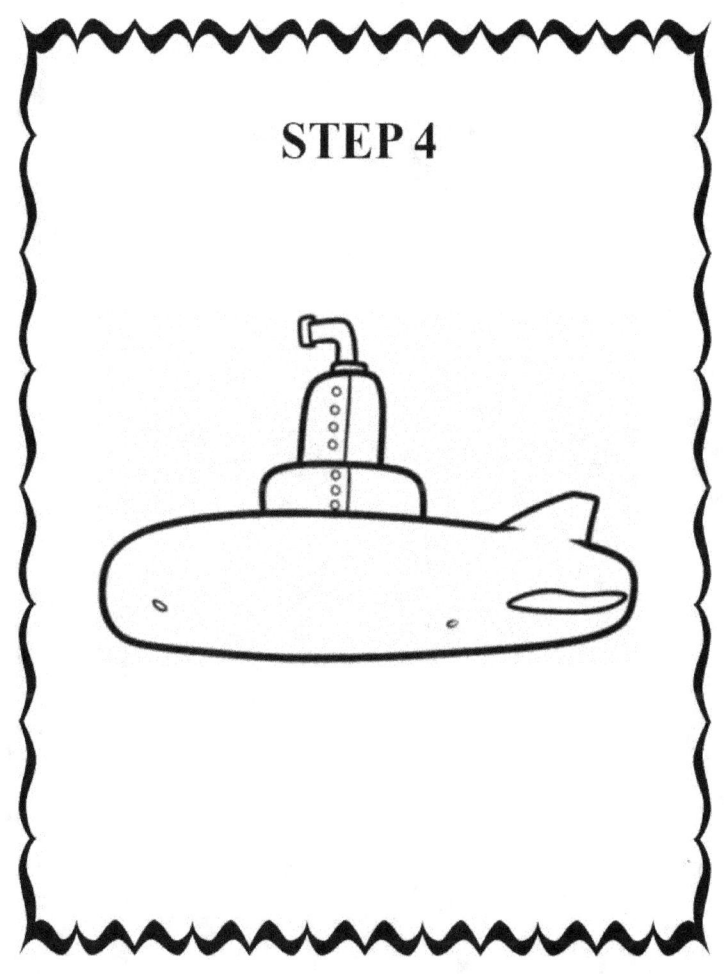

TRACTOR

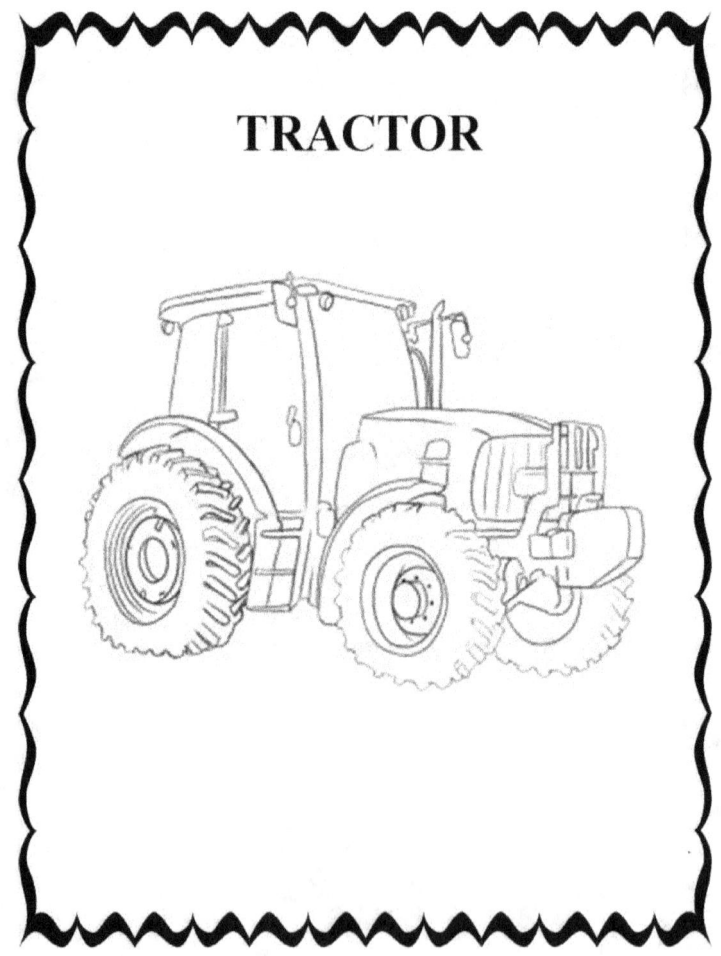

STEP 1

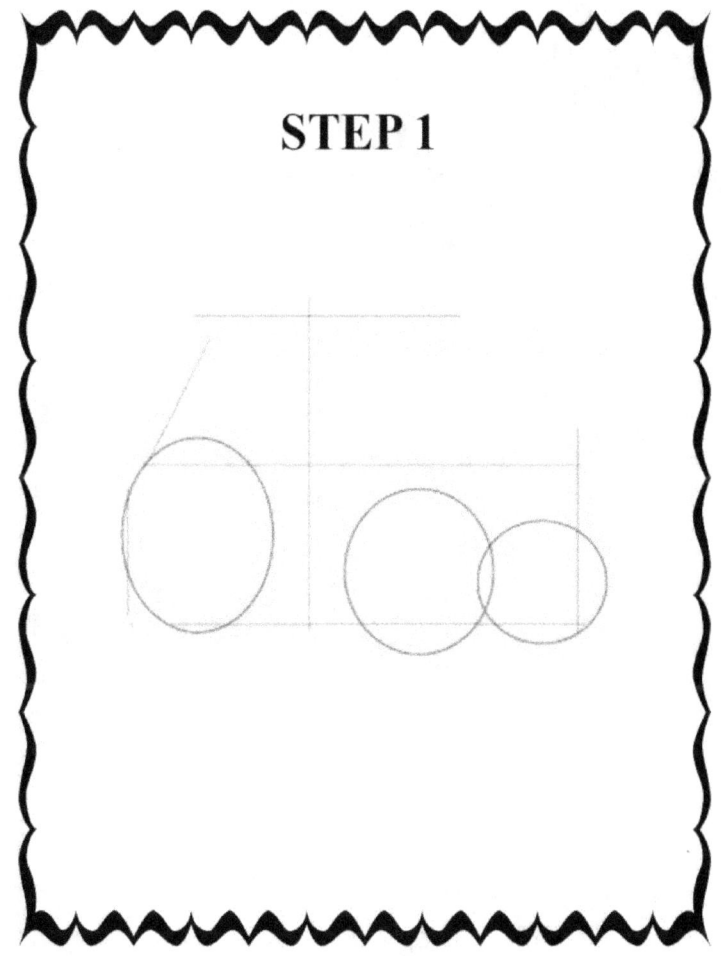

STEP 2

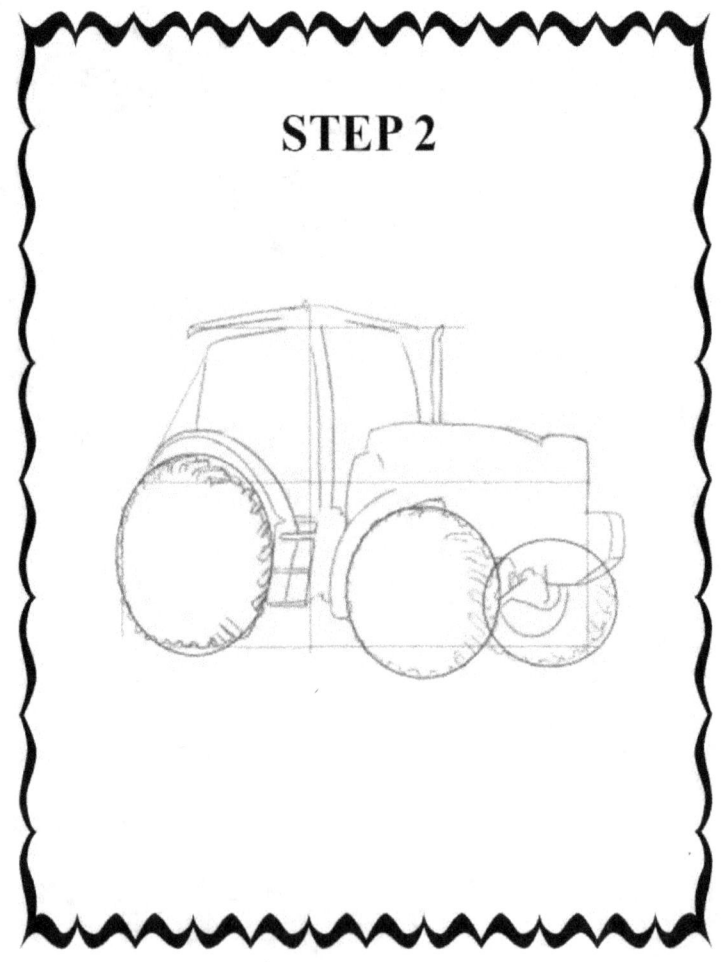

STEP 3

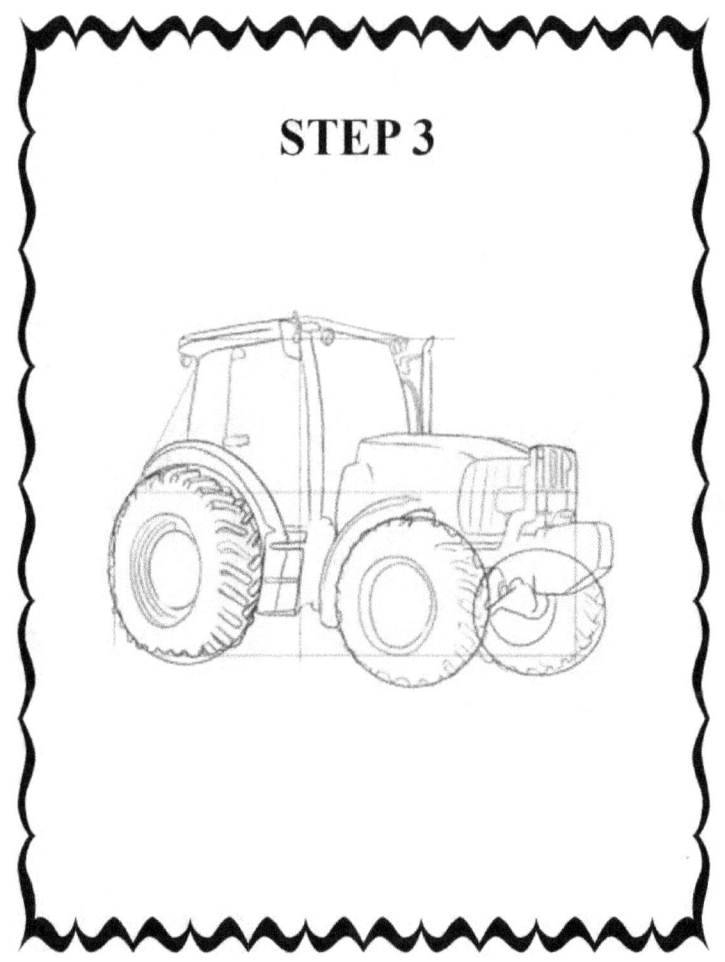

STEP 4

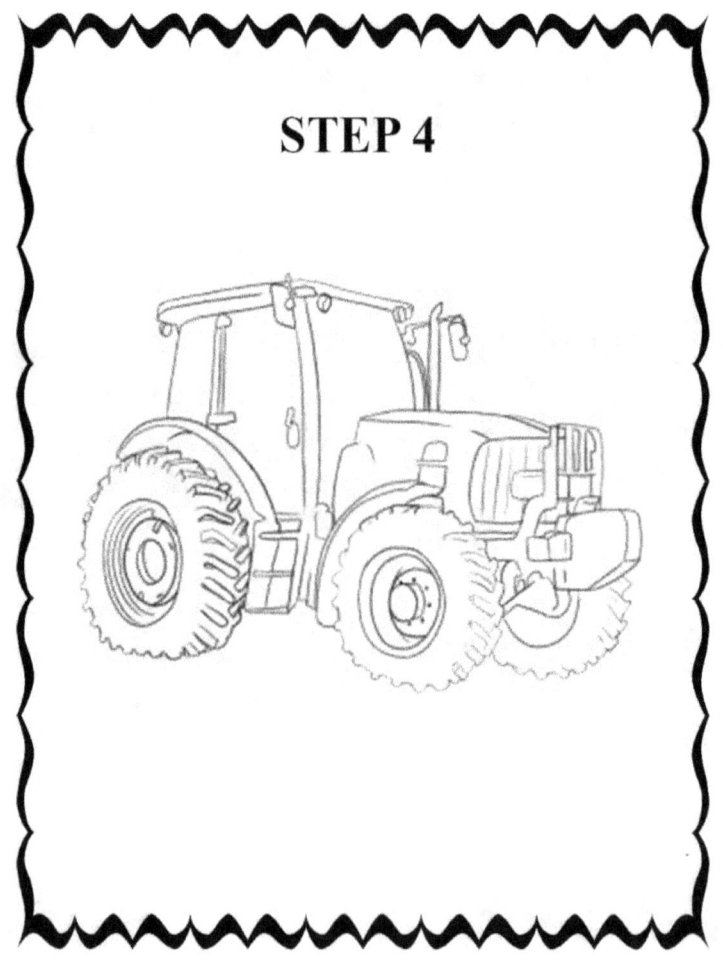

www.ingramcontent.com/pod-product-compliance
Lightning Source LLC
Chambersburg PA
CBHW072029190526
45166CB00015B/1341